The Wines of Languedoc-Roussillon

The World's Largest Vineyard

The Wines of Languedoc-Roussillon

The World's Largest Vineyard

Liz Berry M.W.

Ebury Press
LONDON

First published 1992 by Ebury Press

an imprint of the Random Century Group

Random Century House
20 Vauxhall Bridge Road
London SW1V 2SA

A JILL NORMAN BOOK

A catalogue record for this book is available from the British Library

ISBN 0 09 175361 9

Designed by Rowan Seymour
Set in Ehrhardt by SX Composing Ltd, Rayleigh, Essex
Printed and bound in Singapore by Kyodo Printing

To Mike, without whose patience, encouragement and chauffeuring this book would not have been possible.

Contents

Acknowledgements

I would like to thank Mike for his help, from tasting and searching out samples to proof reading. Thanks to Jill Norman for her constant encouragements and instructive criticism and help in forming this book. Thanks also to the many growers and producers in the Languedoc-Roussillon who have shared their wines, their time and their enthusiasm, and for making the wines which have inspired this book. Thanks to all the La Vigneronne customers who have shared our enthusiasm for the wines of this underrated region. Last and not least, a very special thank you to David and Bridget Pugh for introductions to producers, and for initiating many discoveries at their wonderful restaurant Le Mimosa, where we first tasted many of the best wines of the region.

Preface

Think of the Midi, and most people think of baking sun relentlessly beating down on an endless vista of plains and hillsides, specked with vines and olive trees. A slow, gentle pace of life, and '*gros rouge*' drunk from cheap returnable litre bottles. Much of Languedoc-Roussillon is indeed one vast vineyard, covering some 170,000 hectares of vines, over a third of France's total vineyard area. To put this in perspective, this area's production is far larger than that of many entire countries – Australia, the USA or even Argentina, for example. It is by far the most prolific wine region of France, producing over 33 million hectolitres of wine a year.

But size isn't everything. The problem is that most of the wine is thin, dilute stuff, completely lacking any character. It is usually upon these wines that the region as a whole is judged, and it is because of these wines that the region has gained its reputation as the producer of France's wine lake, sacrificing quality in order to produce vast quantities.

Now, however, the vineyards of the Midi are in a tremendous state of change and improvement, more so than elsewhere in France. Changes in technology and wine-making styles are perhaps more in line here with some of the New World wine countries such as California or Australia. Vineyard land is relatively inexpensive in this part of France, and both French and overseas companies are investing heavily in the region as a result. This is a very exciting region, with huge, state-of-the-art modern wineries and small, traditional growers working side by side to improve the image of their region's wines. Increasing use of quality grape varieties, both traditional and new to the region, is leading to the production of many excellent new wines, and Languedoc-Roussillon is seen increasingly as the vineyard region of the future.

Some Statistics

Only around 10 per cent of the wine produced in Languedoc-Roussillon is AOC (Appellation d'Origine Contrôlée) or VDQS (Vins Délimités de Qualité Supérieure) and some 27 per cent is Vins de Pays. This leaves a balance of over 60 per cent, comprising inexpensive and often undistinguished table wines. This is the area that supplies nearly all of France's branded wines, including the wines from Chantovent, Le Vieux Pâpe and Margnat.

Individual areas have been fighting hard to up-grade their VDQS status to full Appellation Contrôlée, and are therefore very conscious of the overall quality image of the wines in their region. There are now only two VDQS regions within Languedoc-Roussillon, a number of others having been deservedly upgraded in 1985.

There is now a move to sub-divide some of the current regions, which cover large and diverse areas. If the producers within a relatively small area share the same aims, there is no doubt that the quality image of that area can be greatly enhanced, as has happened in St-Chinian, Faugères and Fitou, for example. However, Corbières and Coteaux du Languedoc, which cover very large regions with many wine-makers, have more of a problem. Quality fluctuates from poor and dull to outstanding. Wine-buyers are aware of these areas because of the sheer volume of production, but wide quality variations outweigh this advantage.

France is the largest consumer of Languedoc-Roussillon wines, accounting for some 85 per cent of sales. However, in France as in other wine-drinking countries around the world, styles and fashions in drinking are changing; consumers are increasingly selecting quality at the expense of quantity. Per capita consumption of quality wines (AOC, VDQS and Vins de Pays) is increasing at the expense of table wines (Vins de Consommation Courante). Changing lifestyles, increased concern over alcoholism and health in general, and a growth in customer awareness of wine quality have led to this change. A French government survey showed that whereas in the 1960s two-thirds of consumers would choose a brand rather than an appellation, this had reversed in the 1980s, with the majority preferring to spend slightly more, and to opt for a wine with an appellation.

A rapidly rising trend is in the production and sales of Vins de Pays, a sort of half-way house between ordinary table wines and Appellation Contrôlée wines, and an area where some of the best-value and often highest-quality wines can be found, allowing for more innovative and less restrictive wine-making practices than the more rigid appellation laws.

Thus we are seeing an increase in technical know-how, and in the number of producers bottling their own wines. The higher-quality wines produced by the many co-operatives in the region are also increasing in number.

Since 1986 worldwide sales of Languedoc-Roussillon wines have increased by 20 per cent, and in the United Kingdom this increase has been 43 per cent. West

Germany is currently the largest export market, the United Kingdom following, then Belgium, Holland and Denmark. The USA is starting to take an interest, especially in the finer estate-bottled wines and in good quality varietal wines. As interest increases both in soundly made inexpensive wines and in quality wines at a reasonable price, the export potential for the region is excellent, and probably unrivalled either in France or abroad.

Where to Buy the Wines

Not all the wines mentioned in the book are available in all export markets, and many of the smaller estates are quite hard to come by even in France. Many sell their wines only at the cellar door, or to a few small local restaurants or shops. Most producers, both large and small, are very hospitable, however, and are more than happy to let potential customers taste their wines. Even customers clutching a fistful of francs, and knowing exactly what they wish to buy, are likely to have a glass or three thrust into their hands to taste and enjoy.

A visit to Banyuls one hot summer's day to collect samples for a tasting was therefore quite memorable. Each producer had an average half a dozen wines, all sweet and fortified, and in most cases there was no sign of a spittoon, or even a pot plant. With the producer standing over us, beaming proudly and clutching the next bottle that he wished to show and knew we would enjoy, we drained our glasses. In one Rivesaltes property, where we were tasting the producer's twenty-five-year-old Grenache, a group of students entered carrying a 5-litre plastic *bidon* to be filled with Muscat. They, too, had to experience the Grenache before the producer sold them their Muscat.

The general philosophy of the region is that if the customers like the wines they will buy, but there is very little 'hard sell'. Most producers are happy to sell single bottles to passing tourists, and are open for sales every day of the week. At smaller domaines, however, it is wise to telephone beforehand, otherwise the whole family may be out working in the vineyards.

Languedoc-Roussillon is not a region that calls for much detailed discussion of rare old vintages around the dinner table, nor a region that will delight the classic wine snob. The doting father is unlikely to lay down a fine cellar of Languedoc-Roussillon wines for his baby son to enjoy in twenty years' time, and all too often I hear the comment, '. . . But I couldn't possibly serve that to my guests at a dinner party.' It is, however, a region of outstanding interest for those who enjoy drinking wine and are fascinated by wines and by wine-makers. There are perhaps more discoveries to be made here than in the great wine regions of France. Above all, it is a region of infinite variety, and its best wines are not only readily available both in France and abroad, but they are also affordable.

For a selection of wines from many of the best domaines in the region, with a choice of older vintages no longer available at the property, there is an excellent wine shop, Les Caves d'Occitanie, at 100 rue du Figuerolles, Figuerolles, 34000 Montpellier (tel: 67 27 44 71).

The Geographical Position of Languedoc-Roussillon

Although the Languedoc and Roussillon vineyards are adjacent, the two regions have many differences in topography, climate, geography, history, and gastronomy. We shall be looking at the individual regions and the differences in detail, but there are also many generalizations that apply to the area as a whole. This is the region known as the Midi, and is responsible for much of France's wine lake.

The grouping of the two regions is largely a matter of linking areas with a common wine problem, and is also convenient for tourist promotion. The gastronomy varies greatly from east to west: while Languedoc cuisine is more akin to that of Provence, Roussillon's food shows a strong Catalan influence. Within each region there are also tremendous differences in styles of wine and viticulture.

Languedoc covers the three *départements* of Aude, Gard and Hérault. Roussillon is much smaller, covering the southern part of the *département* of Pyrénées-Orientales, from north of Perpignan to the Spanish border. Thus the combined regions cover wines from the lower reaches of the Rhône, near the towns of Arles and Beaucaire, spreading westwards to encompass the entire Mediterranean coastline from the Rhône to the Pyrenees and the Spanish border, as far north as Carcassonne, the Massif Central and Nîmes.

Languedoc-Roussillon is the largest wine region in the world, with some 170,000 hectares of vines: 35 per cent of France's total vineyard area. It is the most prolific wine region of France, producing over 33 million hectolitres of wine a year, including both quality and table wines. The production is far larger than that of many entire countries – Australia, the USA or even Argentina, for example. Over 60 per cent of its production consists of inexpensive table wines, and it is usually upon these that the region as a whole is judged. It is because of these wines that the region has gained its reputation as the producer of France's wine lake, sacrificing quality in order to produce quantity.

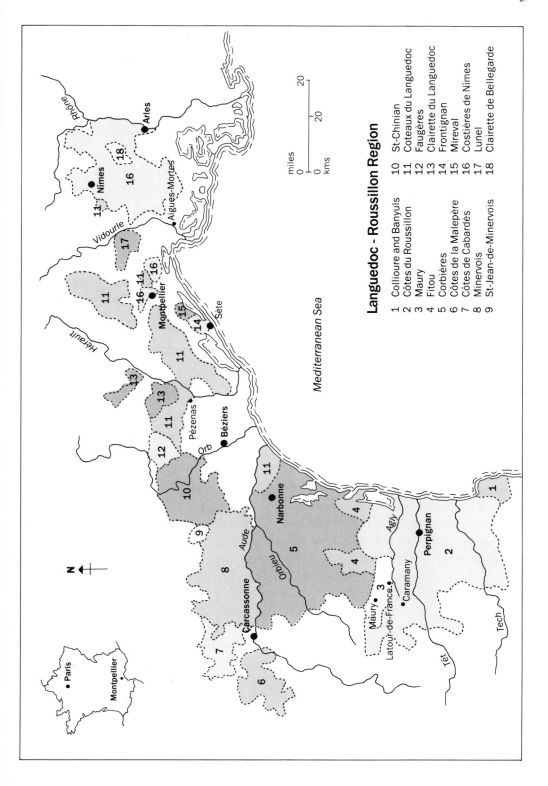

Languedoc - Roussillon Region

1	Collioure and Banyuls	10	St-Chinian
2	Côtes du Roussillon	11	Coteaux du Languedoc
3	Maury	12	Faugères
4	Fitou	13	Clairette du Languedoc
5	Corbières	14	Frontignan
6	Côtes de la Malepère	15	Mireval
7	Côtes de Cabardès	16	Costières de Nîmes
8	Minervois	17	Lunel
9	St-Jean-de-Minervois	18	Clairette de Bellegarde

I

Some History

Vines were probably first cultivated in Languedoc-Roussillon about 500 years BC, at the same time as the introduction of olive trees into France. Languedoc, derived from '*la langue d'oc*', was the name given to the whole southern region of France, where the inhabitants said '*oc*' rather than '*oïl*' to signify 'yes'. Vines were probably imported from Asia Minor by the Phocaeans, who settled in Massalia (Marseilles). Roussillon may have been planted in Roman times, when the region was known as Vicus Russulus, or Red Mountain.

The Mediterranean coast of France proved to be an excellent viticultural area, and was soon widely planted with vines. In AD 92 the emperor Domitian forbade further planting of vineyards and ordered the grubbing up or abandoning of half the area under vine in the provinces, which had taken to viticulture at the expense of wheat and other necessary crop production. This pattern of overproduction followed by official planting restrictions has existed from the first century to the present day.

Rosselló, as Roussillon was known in Catalan, belonged to Spain until the Pyrenees treaty of 1642, and its wines followed the styles and grape varieties found in the rest of Catalonia until this time. It was part of the kingdom of Navarre, and the wines were sold within their own region and in Spain.

The wines of Languedoc-Roussillon were unknown in northern France until several centuries later than those of Bordeaux and Burgundy. Lack of transport routes made it impossible to send the wines that far. Sea routes started at the end of the thirteenth century, but these were slow and costly, and the wines were unlikely to compete in price with trade from the ports of Bordeaux and La Rochelle. The river route via the Rhône was controlled by the powerful wine-producing Rhône and Burgundy regions, which taxed heavily any 'foreign' wines travelling through their territories. The high cost of transport and the long distances limited the market, and until the eighteenth century liqueurs, spirits and special wines were more likely to be transported than table wines. Even in Paris it was only in the seventeenth century that Languedoc-Roussillon wines started to appear.

The port of Sète opened in 1670, and the Canal des Deux Mers, linking the Garonne to the Mediterranean, in 1681. This allowed easier access for Rhône and Languedoc wines through French territory to the port of Bordeaux and the Atlantic, via Toulouse. In facilitating exports, the canal increased wine production in the region. Exports increased via Bordeaux, despite high taxes. Sales to Toulouse were also good. In 1731 a council decree recognized the sale of wine as a major source of income for tax payments in Bas Languedoc.

Many wine-producing cities, including Montpellier and Perpignan, protected their own produce by prohibiting or heavily taxing wines from outside their own region, especially as transport improved.

In 1709 the *grand hiver* frost in January destroyed large tracts of vineyards throughout France, killing many vines and ensuring little or no harvest for at least five years. The southerly vineyards of Provence and Languedoc-Rousillon did not suffer nearly as badly as vineyards further north, and their wines were eagerly welcomed. The government temporarily lowered all internal duties on these wines, as Paris was in need of supplies. This started a precedent: 1725 saw another poor vintage in the Île-de-France region, and once again the King halved taxes on Languedoc wines for a year. Bad vintages occurred quite frequently in the next few decades, and *vignerons* from the Midi saw a promising new market developing for their table wines, especially with the increased use of wine by all classes of society at this time. New areas were planted, and the value of wines more than doubled. These new areas were, however, limited by law to arid soils suitable for quality wine production, to prevent vines from replacing necessary but less lucrative crops such as grain.

Vine-growing began to accelerate further in 1765, after a dearth of wine throughout France caused by a series of poor vintages. Parts of the *garrigue*, or scrubland, were planted, and even some cultivated land. Increased planting led to a surplus of wine, and edicts were passed forbidding new plantations throughout France and also ordering vines planted since 1700 on land not historically intended for vines to be removed. Enforcement depended on the honesty and the judgement of arbitrators, who might be persuaded to decide that the land was 'unfit to be planted with grain', even on fertile plains. Noble landowners complained that it was for them to decide the best use for their land, and vineyards continued to grow despite official protests.

Basville, a commissary in Languedoc, wrote in the 1700s: 'In 1580 there were six times fewer vines in Languedoc than there are at present.' He commented that the increase seemed to be going out of control.

Until the 1750s vine-growing had mainly been in the hands of small proprietors and labourers. By the end of the 1700s, although most properties were still small, many vines were planted on fertile land unsuited to quality wine production. Wine mania had reached the whole region, and every worker had his small plot of vines. In poor soils the yield was an average of 15.5 hectolitres per hectare, just above the national average for the time of 15 hectolitres. In richer, more fertile soils the yield was far greater. Around this time larger properties were planted, with a bigger scale of production than hitherto, and increased yields. On the eve of the Revolution, Languedoc accounted for 10 per cent of French production, compared to about 44 per cent at present.

Prices reached a peak in the 1770s, then fell just before the Revolution, sales falling rapidly by some 30 per cent. A crisis followed, with wine prices falling dramatically to half their previous value because of surplus production. Large, poor quality crops in 1780, '81 and '82 exacerbated the problem. In 1816 Jullien listed 39,526 hectares of vines in Roussillon alone, and wine production from southern France was at a very high level.

Until the early 1800s transport was by road and river, and although the roads were much improved at the beginning of the century, road transport was still slow and very costly. Transport by water was preferred for heavier goods, including wine, although problems of drought or ice could cause delays. Often wines and spirits were sent via Sète, round to the Atlantic ocean via Gibraltar, and up to Paris through the Seine estuary, rather than through the often unreliable internal river and canal system. (1837, 200 boats bringing wine by river to Paris were stranded at the entrance to the Canal de Bourgogne because of empty locks.)

In 1816 Jullien wrote that the main commercial centre in Languedoc was Sète, where *négociants* had houses and shops. In peacetime the offices of Dutch, Danish, Swedish, German, American and English merchants were all to be found in Sète, where they bought their *eaux-de-vie* and wines. Jullien also wrote that Sète had a big trade in producing 'Madeira'! There was an *eau-de-vie* market every Saturday at Pézenas, which influenced the prices in all of Europe. In addition, at this time there was a liqueur market every Friday in Béziers, buying and selling through *négociants* on commission, or through courtiers.

The UK imported many wines, including the fortified wines of the region, and names such as Lunel, Frontignan and Rivesaltes may be found on cellar records of the last century.

In 1848 Hérault overtook the Gironde as the largest area of vines per *département* for the first time, a position which it has maintained ever since. Until the mid nineteenth century a large percentage of the production was distilled, but by then demand for wine was growing, while demand for spirits was decreasing as those from other regions appeared on the market.

The railways radically changed the price and speed of transport, more than halving freight costs. In 1858 a direct rail link from Paris to the south was built. A cask of wine, which had cost 50 francs to transport from Montpellier to Lyon in 1840, could now be transported for a mere 10 francs. Because of the speed of rail, perishable goods such as fruit and vegetables, and lighter styles of wines, could travel from the provinces to Paris for the first time.

The amount of wine produced escalated with the opening of the railway lines, and grape varieties were chosen for quantity rather than quality. The plains were widely planted, and growers banded together to produce larger quantities from collective vineyard holdings. Yields of 80-90 hectolitres per hectare were reported, compared to 20 or 30 from the quality vine varieties planted on hillside vineyards.

Before the coming of the railways, there had been vineyards throughout France, except in the extreme north. Each region was self-sufficient. As cheap wines became available from the south, the less suitable northern vineyards were planted with cereals and sugarbeet instead. In 1868 a journalist in the *Messager du Midi* commented that it was so cheap to produce wine in the south that even after paying transport and taxes Midi wine was as cheap as anything from the north, and that a southern French grower could make more money from unsuitable vineyard soil than could be made from the very finest vineyard sites in the north of France.

During the first half of the nineteenth century France was essentially an agricultural country, although there was growth in the urban population, including the main towns of Languedoc-Roussillon. The industrial revolution brought about a rapid growth of townships, and led to an increased demand for wine in urban centres. Consumption increased with wealth.

At the start of the twentieth century, wine merchants who had been short of wines to sell after the onset of phylloxera had started experimenting with *vins de sucre* – concocted wines that had little to do with grapes or with quality. It became common practice to add sugar and water to the fermenting grape juice to increase yields.

After severe frosts in 1906, little wine was produced in Languedoc-Roussillon and it was hard to obtain a good price for what there was. *Vignerons* pleaded poverty, and were unable to pay their government taxes. A growing mood of dissatisfaction caused growers to group together as the Fédération Viticole, under the leadership of Marcellin Albert a vine-grower from Argelliers, who became their spokesman.

In the spring of 1907, 80,000 protesters from Aude, Pyrénées-Orientales and Hérault marched on Narbonne to protest. In May the Fédération protesters numbered 180,000 at Perpignan, followed by 250,000 at Carcassonne and at Nîmes, and rising to between 600,000 and 700,000 in Montpellier in June.

Georges Clémenceau, president of the council, sent 10,000 troops to stop these protests. The inhabitants put up blockades; many of the soldiers were sons of local vine-growers, who refused to obey army rules and deserted. The remainder of the troops refused to meet a delegation from the vine-growers, and soldiers charged the protesters, then fired on the crowd. Four civilians were killed and fifteen wounded in the shooting. The soldiers had to be withdrawn to the outskirts of the town before order could be restored. The outrage caused revolts in other towns, and many of the local soldiery deserted.

Marcellin Albert went to Paris to discuss the vine-growers' problems, but many felt that he had backed down too soon, and had betrayed them. At the end of 1907 a law was passed to suppress frauds in wine-making, one of the first steps in a series of laws on wine production which were incorporated in the regulations of the INAO (Institut Nationale des Appellations d'Origine) in 1936.

Phylloxera and Other Vineyard Pests

Various natural scourges have appeared from time to time over the centuries to attack the vine. One of the earliest serious vineyard pests was pyrale, a moth that lays its eggs on the young vine shoots and whose caterpillars feed on the young vine growth. It had been present in Languedoc-Roussillon since 1750, and no treatment was found until 1837. Before that time one of the vineyard tasks had been to remove the caterpillars by hand.

Oïdium was the next major problem, appearing in Languedoc in the summer of 1851. Coming from America, it first appeared in greenhouse vines in Margate in 1845. Oïdium is a fungus, *Uncinula necator*, also known as powdery mildew. It affects all the green parts of the vine, giving a greyish powdery appearance and arresting growth, preventing the young grapes from maturing and causing them to split. In 1853 and 1854 oïdium caused severe problems, especially in the hotter, more humid climates south of Charente, which were ideal for its development. In some areas there was no crop at all, in others only a third or a quarter of the usual yield. The Hérault *département* production went from 3,943,000 hectolitres in 1850 to 1,629,000 hectolitres in 1854. Oïdium was soon brought under control, however, by the use of powdered sulphur.

During the Second Empire in France, American vines such as Jacquez had been introduced to the vineyards of Languedoc, for viticulturists to experiment with vine crosses in the search for larger yields and for mildew resistance. In 1863 French vineyards started to display disturbing symptoms: vines yellowed, wilted and died. Research found that the cause was a small aphid, *Dactylospharea vitifolii*, otherwise known as *Phylloxera vastatrix*. The louse feeds on the roots and leaves of the vine, burrowing into the root system and eventually killing the vine. The process was slow at first, and by 1867 only a few communes in Hérault were affected as the louse spread slowly southward and westward in the direction of the dominant winds. As the spread gathered momentum, the vines of Gard were affected, and then the rest of Hérault. As two of the first French vineyard regions to be affected, Gard and Hérault were the worst hit.

Other French *départements* had time to make preparations. Knowing they would soon be attacked, growers planted more, and accumulated revenue ready for the day when re-planting would be necessary.

Various methods of protection against phylloxera were put forward, and the French government offered an immense reward for the person who came up with a cure – a reward that has never been paid out. Among methods tried were the injection of insecticides into the soil. This required special equipment, was expensive (around 200-400 francs per hectare), and could kill the vines. It could also be very unpleasant for the vineyard worker, as the fumes were particularly noxious.

Another method was winter submersion of the vines under water for at least forty to fifty days, to a depth of 25 centimetres, which kills the over-wintering eggs of phylloxera. Naturally it is practical only on flat, relatively slow-draining soils, with a nearby source of water. It is also expensive, necessitating pumps, sluice-gates, retaining banks, and dykes, and therefore practical only for large domaines. This method led to the development of vineyards on plains near the Vidourle and around Narbonne. One advantage was in decreasing salinity on saline plains, which had hitherto been unsuitable for viticulture and could now be planted.

Sandy soils had no problem with phylloxera, which was unable to burrow effectively. This led to the development of the coastal stretches west of Sète, and of the Camargue, by the Salins du Midi.

Re-planting of vines grafted on to American rootstocks in the late 1800s brought other fungi, in the forms of downy mildew and black rot.

With the arrival of phylloxera, and the subsequent destruction of vineyards, the pattern of re-planting changed the face of Languedoc-Roussillon. The investment was such that the smaller vineyards on the slopes, with low yields, were not thought worth re-planting, and the vineyards were now mainly on the plains. At the beginning of the twentieth century Languedoc-Roussillon was producing vast quantities of inferior wine. It had lost its reputation for quality, and was able to sell only on price.

Wine Styles

In the twelfth century, spiced wines were popular. Flavourings in wine have been popular since Roman days, and the School of Medicine in Montpellier taught students the art of spicing wines. This popularity was probably due in part to the fact that the herbs and spices might disguise any faults or deterioration in the wine. Some of the first exports from the region were of liqueurs, or sweetened, fortified, flavoured wines. The port of Sète was known in the twelfth century for its *eau de canelle et de Cette.*

From as early as the sixth century BC, Roussillon was producing both table wines and *vins de liqueur* – sweet, strong wines. The Mediterranean was the only part of France warm enough to produce the very ripe grapes needed for *vins liquoreux*, wines with sufficient sugar to retain sweetness after fermentation had reached some 15° of alcohol. This style was also made by adding alcohol midway through fermentation, to retain some of the grape's natural sugar. These forerunners of today's Vins Doux Naturels gained popularity in France in the mid fourteenth century; before that time this style of wine was mainly imported to France from Greece, Spain and Cyprus.

The interest in fortified wines increased through the 1400s, with wines such as Setúbal, Málaga, Alicante, Madeira and Canary appearing on the best French tables. By the sixteenth century Frontignan was numbered among the world's best *vins liquoreux*, and was exported to Germany, Holland and England, as well as enjoying considerable vogue in Paris.

By the end of the eighteenth century there was a growth of interest in improving the keeping and travelling properties of wine. Chaptal's *Art de Faire le Vin* was very successful when published in 1801, and several editions rapidly sold out. With progress in wine-making skills, Languedoc wines improved in quality and fetched higher prices. Distillation methods also improved, and Languedoc became one of France's chief producers of *eau-de-vie*.

Eaux-de-vie, or brandy, accounted for very large quantities of local wines. Cognac and Armagnac were not widely seen, and spirits from Languedoc-Roussillon were drunk locally, but were also exported. Between 1750 and 1830 Languedoc's reputation as a producer of *eaux-de-vie* was almost the equal of Charentes. As much, if not more, was produced and exported. However, from 1830 to 1850 Cognac started to take the lead, with the appearance of Crus, such as Grande and Petite Champagne, Borderies, and Fins Bois, while Languedoc concentrated more on the production of table wines.

In the 1800s southern French wines, particularly Corbières, were commonly used to ameliorate wines from better-known regions such as Bordeaux and Burgundy. They were popular with blenders because they improved the body and strength of these wines without altering their style and flavour too much. They were shipped in bulk, blended with the better-known wines, and sold under the better-known names. This was another reason why the wines took longer to gain recognition in their own right.

The Birth of Technology

In the nineteenth century the French bourgeoisie invested their new-found wealth in vineyards, and in improving viticultural and vinification techniques. In 1858, at the Exposition de l'Industrie, des Beaux-Arts et des Sciences Naturelles, held in Montpellier, these large estates walked off with all the top prizes. Mixed planting with other crops, or 'polyculture', was replaced by fields devoted to vines, or 'monoculture'. The large properties experimented with different vine varieties, pruning and training methods, improved viticultural practices, cures for maladies and new planting techniques. The vine was developed more intensively, and wine-making became more scientific. Whereas manures and fertilizers had seldom been used on vineyards before the Revolution, and indeed had at times been banned, these were now used to give a larger yield. Growers kept sheep in order to provide the manure for their vines.

At this period high-yielding varieties were introduced, such as Aramon and Terret-Bourret, along with high-alcohol varieties such as Carignan. High-yielding hybrids with good colour, such as Alicante Bouschet and Grand Noir de la Calmette, also became popular. For the first time wine-makers were very dependent on national market forces, no longer merely supplying the local market.

In the middle of the last century Languedoc-Roussillon was at the forefront in wine and vineyard technology, accounting for many improvements, and introducing many new implements to French wine-making.

2

The Commercial Structure

Four out of five growers either belong to co-operatives, or sell to *négociants*. These two groups account for two-thirds of all wine produced in the region. In addition, 80,000 growers who produce their own wine belong to marketing organizations, which help with promotional activities, advice and sales. Sixty per cent of growers own less than 5 hectares, and only 25 per cent have over 50 hectares. Thus the entire region is composed of numerous smallholdings, co-existing with a number of large wine estates. A census in Hérault in 1979 concluded that 36 per cent of vineyard owners had another full-time job, 30 per cent were retired, and only 34 per cent of the growers worked full-time as wine-growers.

Négociants

A *négociant* is a commercial wine company which does not deal exclusively in the produce of its own vines. A *négociant* might own vineyards, but also buys in grapes, grape must, or wine from a number of different sources. Some *négociants* prefer to buy the newly-picked grapes, to ensure that the whole wine-making process is controlled by their company. They will have the necessary equipment to process the grapes, and can be certain that the processing is correctly carried out. They will need cellars located close to the vineyards whose produce they are buying, as grapes start to deteriorate almost the minute they are picked, and any long delay between picking and processing will be detrimental to the wine. If the sources of supply are widely scattered throughout the region, the *négociant* will probably buy wine rather than grapes, as this is a more stable commodity to transport. By selling to a *négociant*, growers have the advantage of a lump sum for some or all of their wine, with none of the financial worries of bottling and marketing the finished product.

A grower may be under contract to supply the *négociant*: he contracts to supply grapes of a certain standard, while the *négociant* contracts to pay a set sum for the produce. A long-term contract from a reliable *négociant* can be invaluable in arranging a bank loan for the grower. Wines may also be bought from growers or from co-operatives on a one-off basis, if the *négociant* is seeking a particular style or appellation for his list.

There are a number of very large *négociants* in Languedoc-Roussillon, with as many variations in quality and style as are found among growers and co-operatives. Usually *négociants* deal with large volumes of very low-profit wines, selling principally to supermarket chains and to wholesale wine companies. Most of the 'own label' wines from this region of France to be found on supermarket shelves both in France and abroad will have been purchased from a *négociant*.

Many *négociants* also supply wines in plastic bottles, which are replacing the French returnable litre '*etoile*' bottle. They may also sell wine in bag-in-box or tetrabrik cartons. These alternatives to the glass bottle are suitable only for wines that will be consumed soon after 'bottling', as the wine will deteriorate more rapidly. They provide cheaper packaging, especially taking into account the expense of transporting the traditional glass bottle. A 1.5-litre plastic bottle of wine weighs around 500 grams, as against around a kilo for a glass 1.5-litre bottle. They also take up less space for transport and for storage, and are becoming increasingly popular, especially in France, where the length of time between bottling and consumption is quite short.

A problem for the *négociants* is the price-versus-quality war. It is hard for the consumer to appreciate the difference between a bottle of Corbières at around 8 francs on the supermarket shelf, and another bottle of Corbières, perhaps with a different-coloured label, at about 12 francs. Without the benefit of an estate name, and with a vast number of proprietary labels in circulation, the consumer has no indication apart from price on which to make a decision. Neither the grower nor the *négociant* gains sufficiently from any improvement in quality, and the emphasis is definitely on low prices. Professional marketing of a quality image for the *négociant* is the only solution, although this also adds several more centimes to the cost of each bottle.

Propriétaires

A *propriétaire* is a grower who owns his land, grows his own grapes, vinifies and bottles his own wine. There are a number of different terms that might be found on the label: *propriéteur-viticulteur*, or owner-vine-grower; *vigneron*, or wine-maker; *viticulteur-récoltant*, or vine-grower-picker; *propriéteur-éléveur*, or proprietor-grower, and *exploitant* or *manipulant*, where the grower rents rather than owns the land, tends the vines and makes the wine, 'exploiting' the patch of land under his control.

A wine made by a private grower or estate is seen as having a certain cachet. The wine is likely to show more individual character than a co-operative or *négociant* wine that may have been blended from a variety of sources. It is easier to pin down than a rather nebulous generic wine, since the bottle carries the wine-maker's name and address rather than a *négociant* or co-operative address. The wine will often have a château or domaine name, which is always reassuring for the consumer. However, the magic words '*mise du domaine*' or '*mise du château*' on the label can still apply to a co-operative wine, where the domaine or château belongs to one or more members of the co-operative and the wine from their property has been vinified separately. The same applies to wines vinified separately by a *négociant*.

Propriétaires vary, in quality, size of domaine, and style of wine, to the greatest extent of the three groups. Some small family estates have very few hectares of vines, probably rented rather than owned, and with only the most basic, old-fashioned wine-making equipment. Other estates cover several hundred hectares, with very modern equipment, temperature-controlled fermentation tanks and new wooden *barriques*. Many estates lie somewhere between the two. A *propriétaire* may not have the money or the space for his own bottling line, and there are several companies who rent out mobile bottling equipment, along with oenological advice if desired. A *propriétaire* is often more flexible in his wine-making approach than a co-operative or a *négociant*, as he can select the best grapes from the best part of his land, and make as many small experimental *cuvées* as he wishes.

Most of the highest-quality wine in Languedoc-Roussillon comes from within this group, but this is also the group that produces much of the poorest quality. Some *propriétaires* are less technically competent than they should be, and wines can still occasionally be found that are oxidized, dirty, or poorly made. A *négociant* or co-operative, on the other hand, will have the benefit of one or more trained oenologists to care for their wine.

Co-operatives

Co-operatives were first formed to help market the wines from groups of growers, and then expanded their scope to vinify, bottle and sell their members' wines. Co-operatives now produce and market over 60 per cent of the total output of the region. Members can benefit from jointly-owned machinery, such as mechanical harvesters, and also have the benefit of advice from trained viticulturalists. With the start of the co-operatives, small growers no longer had to have barrels, casks, bottling facilities, or any other cellar equipment. They became grape farmers, delivering their grapes to the door of the co-operative, and receiving a proportion of the eventual profits from the wine. Growers usually receive a 'share' in their co-operative. When the grapes are delivered to the co-operative, they are weighed, tested for sugar and acid content, and the variety is noted. The grower receives payment according to the quantity and quality of grapes. Some co-operatives are much more particular than others, and have devised a 'points system' for variety, yield, age and health of vines and grapes, and analysis of the grape must.

The first co-operative, Les Vignerons Libres, was started at Maraussan in Languedoc. Between 1900 and 1907 thirty *co-opératives de vente* had been set up, marketing the wines produced by their members. The uneven quality of the wines led to the co-operatives taking a more important role in the wine-making process. By 1914 there were 217 co-operatives in France, but the real growth came after the Second World War, and now there is one in practically every small village in Languedoc-Roussillon. In 1946 the Institut Co-opératif du Vin was created to help oenological progress and to advise co-operatives with their investment. Co-operatives now vinify between 60 and 70 per cent of the region's total output. They vary considerably in quality, some providing innovative high-quality wines while others still show a sad lack of understanding of the commercial market.

The co-operative movement is without doubt one of the main influences in the current upsurge in quality wine production within the region, and in many areas accounts for almost 100 per cent of the production. Co-operatives have also carried out much research and marketing of Vins de Pays, and are responsible for increases in sales of these wines.

3

Viticulture

Originally vines were grown as part of a polyculture alongside other crops, each farmer growing sufficient grapes, grain, fruit and vegetables for his own needs and for local sale. As transport systems improved and farmers started to supply wider markets, specialist growers of vegetables, or of vines, started to appear, and fields were planted with a single crop, a monoculture.

Originally vines were planted rather haphazardly: before phylloxera, new vines were formed by *marcottage*, burying the tip of a shoot bent down from a neighbouring vine, and anchoring it in place until roots formed.

Vine Pruning and Training

The vine drops its leaves in winter, and each spring starts growing most strongly from the buds nearest the extremity of the previous year's shoots, so there has always been a system of pruning to keep the vine's shape manageable. Pruning is the annual cutting back to keep the shape, and training is the permanent shape of the vine maintained by pruning.

Vines were traditionally shaped as small bushes, a system of training known as *gobelet*. The vine trunk rose vertically from the ground to a height of between 6 and 12

inches, branching out into a small knob of stems, which were cut back annually. This system was relatively simple for growers to maintain, obviated the need for stakes and wires, protected the vines from the *mistral* and the *tramontane*, strong winds which blow violently through the vineyards at many times of year, and could be used equally on flat vineyard land, on very steep slopes or on terraces. The spread of branches gave good aeration to the vine, helpful in minimizing insect or mildew damage.

Each vine has between three and seven main branches spreading from the central trunk. Earlier this century the central trunk was very short, and the branches quite widely spaced. Now the tendency is for a longer central trunk, and a shorter circle of branches. This makes it easier for the grower to maintain both the soil and the vine. With the arrival of horse-drawn ploughs, and later of tractors, spacing became more even and rows between vines became wider. *Gobelet*-trained grapes cannot be picked by mechanical harvester, and the other disadvantage of the *gobelet* system is the height of the grapes for picking – very low down, and back-breaking for the pickers. As much of the land is still widely distributed between a large number of small family holdings, the bush-shaped vines will continue to be seen quite widely throughout the region.

Other training systems are appearing with the increased use of mechanization, including mechanical harvesters. The traditional *gobelet* has become a flattened *gobelet*, with the branches radiating sideways, in the same direction as the row of vines, in a system known as *évantail*, meaning fan. In this way the grapes can be mechanically harvested, and the vines can be mechanically pruned if wished. A similar system of pruning is the *cordon de royat*, where the vine shape is a trunk with one or two horizontal 'arms', at a height of about 50 centimetres from the ground, from which the year's shoots will appear. This system is also suitable for mechanization. Both these systems need a stake for each vine for the first few years of its life, while its shape is being formed, and the cordon additionally needs a wiring system to support the permanent arms while these are developing. This makes the vineyard initially more expensive than one using the traditional *gobelet* training, but not as expensive as a permanent wiring system.

These systems of training are known as 'spur' pruning – nearly all the wood of the

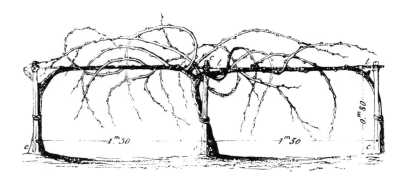

previous year is cut off, leaving several little spurs of two to three buds for the current year's growth. The alternative type of training is 'cane' pruning, where one or more of the previous year's branches or canes are kept, and the current year's growth is from buds along the cane. The most usual cane training system in Languedoc-Roussillon is *Guyot*, where either one or two canes are retained, to be trained horizontally from a central trunk.

One cane is known as single *Guyot*, two as double *Guyot*. Each year the strongest

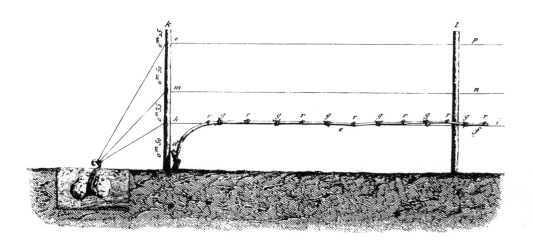

cane from the previous year, nearest to the trunk, is kept, and all other growth removed. This system necessitates a much more expensive system of permanent stakes and wires to support the canes, but is very suitable for mechanization. It is less suitable on steeply terraced vineyards, where the wiring would be impractical. It also requires an element of skill on the part of the pruner in choosing the most suitable canes for the following year.

The system chosen will depend on a number of factors. Apart from the possibility of mechanization, and the steepness of the site, the grower must consider the attributes of the grape variety. Some are naturally more fertile than others, and will need pruning to leave a minimum number of buds or 'eyes', while less fertile varieties need a greater number of eyes to assure a reasonable crop. A grower's opinion of a 'reasonable crop' will also vary considerably. Some varieties with weaker canes will need wire supports to prevent them being snapped off if the vineyard is liable to strong winds. Some growers prefer spur pruning because the cuts or wounds to the vine will be smaller, giving less risk of infection than with a larger wound caused by removing two-year-old wood in cane pruning. The quality can be monitored equally well using either method of pruning.

Vine-growers observed that closely spaced vines gave a better quality crop when the yield from each vine was limited, and the risk of uneven crops caused by maladies to the vine was lessened by the higher number of vines. On the other hand, the initial outlay was more expensive, and work in the vineyard was more difficult. The cost of production was therefore higher than in a vineyard with fewer, more widely spaced vines. The largest variations will be seen on the flat land, which lends itself to mechanization and to irrigation; large expanses of widely spaced trellises can be seen interspersed with more traditionally trained vineyards.

Work in the Vineyard

Apart from the annual pruning or shaping of a vine, there will also be interim pruning during the period of growth, sometimes known as 'green' or summer pruning. This will tidy up the vine, keeping it in shape, and concentrate its energy on grape production. Summer pruning is to some extent optional; it will increase the quality of the yield, and decrease the quantity. Both the labour and the resultant loss of yield will increase the cost of the wine produced, and can only be undertaken where the grower can afford to charge the extra amount on each bottle. For this reason, only a small percentage of growers in Languedoc-Roussillon can afford to practise summer pruning.

Epamprage is the removal of *gourmands*, or non-productive suckers shooting from the main trunk. These may be removed by hand, or by machines that gently scrape the trunk, usually in late May or early June, before the *gourmands* can divert too much energy from the main shoots, and before flowering, which is generally in early June.

Ecimage, the removal of the shooting tips, takes place after flowering. The period of vigorous growth will be almost finished by then, and removal of the tips concentrates the vine's energy on the flowers. This is especially useful in very vigorous varieties, or those that are liable to poor flower set (*coulure*). At least five leaves should be left above flower spurs, to ensure sufficient photosynthesis.

Rognage, the thinning of shoots and leaves, takes place in July or August, allowing better aeration of the vine to eliminate disease and to allow treatment sprays to penetrate more efficiently, as well as facilitating the vintage. In June or July some of the grape bunches may also be removed, to increase the quality in the remaining bunches. This cannot be done until after the flower shoots have set, and the grapes have just started to swell. Too soon, and the remaining bunches will grow bigger to compensate for the loss; too late, and the energy will already have been lost. Once again, only the estates that can afford the costs of a smaller harvest can practise bunch removal.

Effeuillage, leaf-plucking, also takes place in July and August. Leaves are removed from immediately above grape bunches to allow the sun to penetrate, and to minimize the risk of mildew. *Effeuillage* is less widely practised in the south of France than further north, as growers may risk burning the grapes if the sun's rays are too hot. It is sometimes carried out shortly before mechanical harvesting, to eliminate the possibility of leaves being picked along with the grapes.

Grafting and Re-grafting, the Choice of Rootstock

Since phylloxera, almost all vines have had to be grafted on to American rootstocks. *Vitis vinifera*, the species of vine that produces quality wine grapes, has roots that are easily destroyed by phylloxera. American vine species, which are immune to phylloxera, produce grapes with a strong flavour, generally unacceptable for making good wine. The stem and fruiting part of the *Vitis vinifera* variety is grafted on to the root part of the American vine, providing a vine that is both resistant to phylloxera and has the qualities of the *Vitis vinifera* grapes.

There are a number of rootstocks for the grower to choose from, and the choice will have a bearing on the quality of the wine, although to a much lesser degree than the choice of variety. Rootstocks vary in vigour, precocity, resistance to moisture or to drought, and also in resistance to various soil constituents, especially limestone and salt content. The choice of rootstock will depend on the vineyard soil, and also on compatibility with the variety chosen. The grower will decide whether to choose a rootstock that will give a large yield, but maybe a less concentrated wine, or whether to opt for a smaller yield with higher potential quality. A poor choice of rootstock may lead to problems in the vineyard, with over-vigorous vegetative growth or with chlorosis, a condition caused by mineral deficiency or excess, causing the leaves to turn yellow and stop photosynthesizing.

Vineyards on sandy soils do not have the problem of phylloxera, as the louse cannot burrow in very sandy areas, and these vines do not need to be grafted.

The other phenomena that is starting to appear in Languedoc-Roussillon is that of 'grafting over'. This is a process whereby one variety can be transformed into another with the minimum delay. Instead of uprooting the vineyard and re-planting with the chosen variety, the vines are 'T-budded': the fruiting top of the main trunk is sawn off, and a small portion of cane containing a bud of the required variety is grafted on to the top of the stem on each side of the trunk. In this way the root system is left intact, and the vine is back into full production within a couple of years. This is a very useful technique, especially in areas that wish to keep up to date with fashion, and where there are rapid changes in the demand and the price paid for certain varieties.

Re-grafting took place on a large scale in California in the 1970s, when the demand for premium white varieties outstripped supply; the same is happening today in Languedoc-Roussillon, where a much higher price can be obtained for varieties such as Chardonnay, while red Carignan grapes, for example, can hardly pay their way.

Soil, and the Notion of terroir

The French have always been very keen on the notion of *terroir*, that mysterious *je ne sais quoi* which is present in the best classic vineyards of France and which can never be emulated by the upstart vineyards of the New World. *Terroir* is the whole concept of the place where the vines are grown, covering not just the soil structure and texture, but the topography, climate, latitude and other characteristics of the vineyard.

The soil is the medium in which the vine is grown, and needs to provide the vine with everything it needs for a healthy life. Water is the most essential element for the vine's health, and must be provided steadily throughout the growing season, in sufficient quantities to stop the plant from wilting with thirst, but without waterlogging and asphyxiating the roots, which may lie some 2-6 metres below the surface in a mature vine.

Different types of soil have different water-retaining abilities, and good vineyard soil needs to retain sufficient moisture at a depth that can be assimilated by the vine, without waterlogging in times of heavy rainfall. Water retention will depend on the physical properties of the soil, the size and shape of the particles, and the depth to which the roots of the vine can penetrate. This aspect of a vineyard cannot easily be altered artificially, although some estates have machinery that can mince rock up into particles of whatever size is desired, from large stones to fine dust. Château de Jau in Roussillon is creating marvellous vineyard soils from what was almost solid rock.

A good soil will warm up quickly in the spring, to help the vine start budding as soon as possible. This ability depends on the porosity, colour, structure and texture of the soil. Good soils include the round *galets* or pudding stones of the Costières du Nîmes or the Méjanelle region near Montpellier, the angular stony soils around St-Chinian, and the decomposed schist soils around Banyuls. These soils combine the ability to warm up in the spring, to drain off excess water, with a water-retentive subsoil to carry the vine through the hot dry summer months. This is the reason for the quality reputation of the best vineyard regions throughout France; the ability to control any excesses of nature, and to produce an even quality in good and poor vintages alike.

The vine requires certain nutrition from the soil to help feed the leaves and other green parts and to assist in healthy growth. Apart from nitrogen and potassium, the vine will need small doses of iron, boron, phosphorus, magnesium and calcium during the period of growth and of fruit-ripening. The amount of these available, and the vine's ability to make use of them, will depend on the acidity or alkalinity of the soil, and on the organic matter present. All these factors can be added or altered artificially, but a good *terroir* will have a suitable balance, without the need for too much interference.

Fertilization, by means of manure, compost, or chemicals, is a contentious matter. French vineyards are traditionally on poor soil, while many of the New World vineyards are on rich, fertile soil. Fertile soil can cause excessive vegetal growth, the vine producing shoots and leaves rather than concentrating on grape production and ripening. Excessive nitrogen can lead to grapes with lower sugar levels, and to vines with lower disease resistance. Excessive potassium can limit the absorption of magnesium, giving poor fruiting. Fertile soils need to be deeper, allowing the roots to explore more territory to find their natural balance. Having said this, fertilization can greatly increase the size of the crop produced, and therefore the revenue per hectare of land.

In past centuries, vineyards were limited to soils where other crops would not grow, to areas where drought-tolerant herbs such as lavender and thyme were the only plants found. It was forbidden to plant vines on fertile plains, or in rich soils that could be used for corn or vegetables. This was a sensible prohibition; it is generally accepted that vines produce their finest grapes where they have to struggle – not too much, but sufficiently to limit the crop and thereby concentrate the flavour. Fertilization only really started in the last century, when commercial interests became pressing and growers started to think in terms of higher revenue.

The soils of the Midi cover an enormous range of types, from sands and alluvial deposits, through glacial dust and pebbles, to large rocks and stones. There are also areas of clay and of limestone. The best *terroirs* of the Languedoc-Roussillon are without exception those with the longest history of fine wine production. There are some villages that were famous two centuries ago, where wines are no longer produced, which is a shame. These are mainly in areas that have become industrialized or urbanized, for example around the outskirts of Perpignan and Montpellier. There are also large tracts of vineyards where vines were forbidden two centuries ago, which is maybe an even greater crime. It is the wines from some of these latter which debase the production of the whole region, producing the embarrassing lake of cheap table wine that nobody wishes to buy or drink.

It is possible to produce a very passable, well-made and pleasing wine from these fertile plains, and several companies are doing it very well, where sufficient research has gone into planting the correct varieties and processing the wine in the correct manner. The fault lies rather with some of the grape farmers, who churn out the largest possible yields of the most productive varieties, regardless of flavour or quality.

Climate and Microclimate

The climate covers the overall weather conditions of an area; the microclimate is the very localized climate around one vine, although the word is often used to denote an individual vineyard's climate conditions. The macroclimate is the correct term for the individual vineyard. The climate is strongly linked to the latitude, and we can therefore assume that the south of France is 'hot'. However, there are many variations in climate within Languedoc-Roussillon, the heat depending mainly on altitude and proximity to the sea, on prevailing winds, and also to some extent on the slope of the vineyard: hotter facing southwards towards the sun, cooler facing northwards away from the sun. Thus the macroclimate will vary within a very small area, especially where the altitude varies. Mas de Daumas Gassac has recorded temperature differences of around 6°C in the summer months between the vineyards, which are on the higher slopes, and the house, which nestles in the valley. Their vines ripen several weeks later than those in the neighbouring village, whose vineyards are better sheltered from the winds.

Rainfall is part of the climate pattern, and as we have seen, water is the most important aspect of the vine's diet. The majority of the rain falls in the winter months in Languedoc-Roussillon: summer rainfall is low, often spasmodic and uneven. Rainfall varies throughout the region, but is generally on the low side, so the ability of the soil to retain moisture is of great importance, except where irrigation is permitted.

There are strong winds within the region, both the *mistral* and the *tramontane*. These can be a nuisance for the grower, breaking off stems and shoots, but also help greatly in eliminating insect pests and in aerating the vineyard to minimize rot problems. They can cool the climate down, but will also dry the air in summer, accentuating any drought conditions.

Yields – and Why Do They Vary So Much?

The yield, or the amount of wine to be obtained from a hectare of land, varies considerably throughout the region, depending on the soil, the climate and rainfall, the grape variety grown, and the way the vine is pruned. The maximum yield is always stipulated for AC wines, because over a certain quantity the flavour will be diluted and the wine will become less concentrated. This maximum is expressed in hectolitres of grape must per hectare of vines, and it varies from region to region, with an average of around 45-50 hectolitres per hectare across the whole of Languedoc-Roussillon. Vins de Pays are also limited in yield, but to a lesser extent, to around 80 hectolitres on average. If growers over-produce, their entire yield can be declassified to Vin de Table.

There is only a certain quantity of nutrients in the soil, and only a certain amount of water. These factors, together with the available heat from the sun, will affect the amount of grapes that each vine can ripen in a year. Given a high-yielding vine variety, and unlimited fertilization, water and heat, the yield can be as much as 200-300 hectolitres per hectare in southern France, but the wine will be thin, flavourless and without character. A small yield will give more concentrated wine, higher in extract and flavour, and with more character. Although the authorities have laid down legal maxima, usually an even finer wine can be obtained by honing the yield still further, while allowing for economic factors. A very low yield, however, is not necessarily going to produce a better wine all the way down the scale. Below a certain minimum, generally 20-30 hectolitres per hectare in southern France, low yields may be the result of unhealthy or dead vines within a vineyard, or of inefficient vine management. However, as vines age the yield is reduced and the quality increased: very low-yielding old vines often produce a very fine wine. Also, some of the older French vine varieties, dating from before cloning, produce only very small yields of very high-quality wine, as for example Mas de Daumas Gassac's Petit Manseng vines, cuttings taken from very old vines in Jurançon, which produce only between 15 and 20 hectolitres per hectare. Viognier, also, is traditionally a very temperamental grower, giving small yields in most vintages.

Irrigation

Irrigation is the artificial supply of water to a vineyard by means of a series of pipes or canals. In most parts of France, this practice is forbidden for the production of wine grapes. Most of France experiences sufficient rainfall during the growing season for the vine's needs, and the supply of extra water would only augment the size of the crop, probably to the detriment of its quality. In certain areas of southern France the vines would suffer too much from drought without irrigation, and the authorities have permitted growers to supplement the water supply under certain conditions. The watering must stop on 1 August, and a declaration must be made to the director of taxes. By forbidding irrigation after this date, the authorities ensure that water is provided only during the vine's main growing period, and not to augment the crop after the grapes have started to swell.

Only certain stipulated areas are allowed to irrigate, including some areas where the soil would otherwise be too high in salt content, where irrigation helps to cleanse the soil at the same time as providing moisture. Tests are being carried out in Languedoc, monitoring both quality and quantity, with irrigation being supplied in between one and four waterings according to the natural rainfall, at twenty-day intervals from budbreak until 1 August. Usually about 60 millimetres of water is supplied in each watering, providing about 600 cubic millimetres per hectare. Irrigation can also be used to supply fertilization, which is mixed into the water supply.

Mechanization, the Way Forward?

With the increasing costs of manual labour, there is no doubt that mechanization will continue to increase in vineyards throughout France. While the first mechanical harvesters were by no means perfect, technology has improved considerably, and the grapes coming into the cellar are in better condition. Mechanical harvesters can not only replace a large and expensive team of pickers with one experienced driver, but can pick the entire vineyard at the same speed as the pickers. Picking can even be carried out at night, using arc lights, and the grapes can thus be brought into the winery at a cooler temperature than if they had been picked during the day.

Mechanical pruning will also replace a number of man-hours. Attachments rather like hedge-trimmers remove most of the unwanted growth from the vines, and the pruner just has to 'tidy up' what is left.

The Choice of Variety

The choice of grape variety will have a great influence on the flavour and quality of the wine produced. For a wine to receive AOC or VDQS status, the choice of variety is laid down in the laws governing each delimited region. These laws have been formed over the course of the current century, taking into consideration the varieties most commonly found in each region for quality wine production, as well as the soil and climatic conditions of the region. The laws can be more of a hindrance than a help in some instances; the varieties to be found in many parts of Languedoc-Roussillon at the start of the century were not necessarily those that would produce the best wine for the region, and many excellent varieties that had been successfully grown until the end of the last century are excluded from the AC for this reason.

Languedoc was one of the first areas of France to be affected by phylloxera, and so one of the first to re-plant. The growers' motives at the time of re-planting were to choose varieties that would produce grapes reliably each year, with large and regular yields. With other wine regions of France succumbing to phylloxera in their turn, growers saw the opportunity to make a quick buck. Quantity was the order of the day, and not quality.

Flatter vineyard areas were easier and therefore cheaper to re-plant than steep slopes and terraces. The expanses of fertile plain along the river banks were easy to flood in winter, to combat phylloxera, and were extensively planted, while the steep slopes and terraces were largely neglected. Land that had been considered unfit for quality wine production previously was now covered in vines as far as the eye could see. When the INAO examined the region in order to delimit vineyard regions and decide on permitted grapes, it was inevitable that some wrong decisions would be made.

For the Appellation Contrôlée laws, varieties were divided into classes: 'recommended', 'authorized' and 'tolerated'. Tolerated varieties were generally given an ultimatum, a date by which they should be replaced, or after which they could no longer be planted, while recommended varieties were often ordered to be increased proportionally, usually in several stages over a number of years. Authorized varieties might state a maximum percentage for each vineyard to be planted. Usually the tolerated varieties comprised the highly productive but poorly-flavoured vine strains, such as Aramon, that had been planted in the 'get rich quick' era after phylloxera. The authorized or recommended varieties were those most widely planted throughout the Midi: Carignan, Cinsault and Grenache. All three of these varieties have their merits, although familiarity often brings contempt. Recommended plantings included varieties such as Syrah and Mourvèdre, sometimes known as *cépages améliorateurs*; these could improve aroma and flavour in a red wine but had been neglected in many regions for reasons of poor or irregular yield, or similar practical problems not found with the hardier Carignan, Cinsault or Grenache. Some of the better-quality varieties of the eighteenth and nineteenth centuries had not been thought worth re-planting after phylloxera. These did not therefore get listed as permitted AC varieties.

The historian and wine writer Jullien wrote in 1816 that the most widely grown varieties in Roussillon at that date were Grenache, Mataro (Mourvèdre) and Crignane (Carignan). These were the wines most sought for export. Other grape varieties included Picpoul Noir, Picpoul Gris, Terret and Blanquette, making wines with less colour. In some areas one also found St-Antoine, Malvoisie and Macabeo. The famous viticulturist Dr Guyot also studied vine-growing in the region in the 1870s, where experiments had been undertaken for over a century to improve the quality of the grape mix in the vineyards. He mentioned such varieties as Cabernet Sauvignon, Syrah, Cot, Sauvignon and Sémillon, stating that some growers were producing exquisite wines from these varieties, and highly recommending their use. Unfortunately many of these potentially high-quality varieties are excluded under Appellation Contrôlée regulations.

It is possible for new varieties to enter the Appellation Contrôlée system, but only if a large percentage of the local growers are in agreement, and only after lengthy legislation.

Some varieties take longer to ripen their grapes than others, and generally the best wines will be produced where the ripening period takes place over as long a period as possible for the region. Thus northern France is limited to early ripening varieties because of the shorter, cooler growing season, while the south of France can grow a very wide range of varieties in its longer, hotter summer climate. If grapes ripen too quickly in a warmer climate than they need, they risk losing some of the flavour and aroma which would develop during a slower maturation period; thus some fashionable varieties such as Chardonnay, which can ripen by mid-August in the Midi, may not produce a very exciting wine in warmer vineyard sites.

Although the whole of Languedoc-Roussillon is considered a 'hot' region, there are very varied climates from one part to another, and varieties such as Chardonnay may be more at home in cooler, higher-altitude vineyards, or in those whose summer heat is mitigated by sea breezes. Conversely, late ripening varieties such as Mourvèdre will be happier in the warmest vineyard sites.

Since the late 1970s growers have also had the option of Vins de Pays labelling for their wine, and have had permission to plant a number of new and exciting grape varieties which are outside the AC status. This is a tremendously important step forward for the region, and opens the way for experimentation with the world's finest varieties. Increasingly, growers are opting out of the over-restrictive Appellation Contrôlée legislation to produce Vins de Pays from 'prohibited' varieties. Some of the finest wines of the region are among this prohibited group, as are most of the big investment companies' wines.

4

Vinification

At the beginning of the century there was a good market for medicinal wines, industrial flavoured aperitif wines, and *mistelles*, made from grape juice muted with neutral alcohol. The emphasis was on price and not quality. The popular French aperitif wines (St-Raphael, Dubonnet, Noilly Prat) were nearly all produced using base wines from Languedoc-Roussillon. There are still vast quantities of flavourless, innocuous wines produced in the region, but the scope of this book is to seek out the wines of character.

The 'table wines' (normal, unfortified wines) of Languedoc-Roussillon are predominantly red (around 90 per cent), with smaller quantities of rosé and white. The region also produces France's largest proportion of Vins Doux Naturels, fortified wines made from grapes picked with a high degree of ripeness. A small quantity of sparkling wine is also produced.

The quality and style of the wines produced will depend on the wine-maker's expertise, on the grape varieties grown, and on the *terroir* of the vineyard. They will show more character if the yields have been kept to a reasonable level, and if the wine-maker has taken care in the production. Because of the warm climate, Languedoc-Roussillon is one of the easiest parts of France in which to grow grapes, and many growers prefer the option of producing large quantities from varieties that are easy to grow to the more skilled and more risky business of producing small quantities of fine wines.

After the phylloxera scourge, co-operatives began to appear throughout the region. Wine-making became less artisanal and more industrialized. Cement tanks replaced the traditional wooden vessels in cellars, and pumps were introduced to move the crushed grapes to the fermentation vessels, and the finished wine to the maturation vessels. Continuous mechanized presses started to appear, replacing the old wooden presses. The quality of the finished wine could suffer if the handling were too rough and mechanical; harsh tannins and oils could be formed by crushing the stems and pips, and mechanical pumping of the wine around the winery could lead to oxidation, as well as losing the delicacy and aromas of the fruit. In addition, the co-operatives were built in a very different style to the traditional old domaines and châteaux. Many of the co-operatives have a simple, functional design.

Sometimes long queues of tractors with loaded trailers would wait at the co-operative for their turn to be weighed, and to off-load their grapes into the crusher. Growers all wanted to pick over the weekends, when the wife and family would be available to help, although the optimum picking date might well not coincide with the weekend. Grapes might sit in the hot sunshine for several hours in the height of the picking season, and the co-operative had to ensure that its equipment had the capacity to handle the quantity delivered in such a short space of time.

Another former practice was *quitchage*, the pressing down of grapes into the collecting tubs in order to fit the maximum quantity of grapes in on each trip. The crushed grapes would then start the process of decomposition and fermentation in the hot autumn sunshine, long before they arrived at the winery, and all sorts of off-flavours would result from the excessive tannins and volatility.

Many of these technical problems have been ironed out over the last twenty years, as technical competence has greatly improved. There is still room for improvement in some wineries, however.

Unlike the co-operatives, most traditional domaines continued as they had before phylloxera, with older and less sophisticated wine-making equipment. Grapes were pressed in basket presses, and most domaines had little or no temperature control, even if they were aware of its importance. Wine-making techniques were handed on from father to son, with little formal training. Many small domaines lacked finance, and equipment was often primitive.

Sugar content of grapes can be high in the Midi; as the grapes ripen, their sugar content increases, while acidity decreases. Unlike vineyards in cooler regions of France, there is always sufficient sunshine to ripen the grapes fully, and they will remain unripe only if the grower attempts to produce unreasonably large crops. For this reason, chaptalization, the addition of sugar to the grape must to increase potential alcohol, has been forbidden in Languedoc-Roussillon since 1929, although earlier this century *vin cuit*, a sweet wine produced from boiled down grape juice, was sometimes added to red grape must to increase its richness.

Over the last twenty years more emphasis has been placed on quality, and the growers have become more market-orientated. *Foulo-pompes*, which crushed the grapes and pumped them into fermentation vessels, have been replaced by a gentler pump action, or by conveyor belts to take the grapes whole to the vats. With the development of *macération carbonique* (See page 34), continuous presses have been discouraged and replaced by presses with a gentler action. Grapes are now often picked into square plastic crates which can be stacked one on top of another without squashing the grapes below. These are more hygienic, and can be cleaned more easily than the old wooden tubs.

Red Wine Vinification

The juice of most wine-making grapes is white, and the colour is contained in the grape skins. A few of the red varieties grown in Languedoc-Roussillon are *teinturier* varieties, which have red-coloured juice as well as red skins. This is a rare characteristic in *Vitis vinifera*, the European wine-making vine family, and is usually an indication of a hybrid vine, one that has been crossed with a non-*vinifera* vine.

The grapes are lightly crushed to break the skins. Sometimes some or all of the stems are removed, because grape stems can give a wine harsh, bitter, stalky flavours. The grapes are then put in a fermentation vessel which is usually made of wood, lined cement, or stainless steel, where the fermentation commences. Sometimes the natural yeasts present in the form of bloom on the grape skins are left to cause the fermentation, which will happen naturally once the grape skins are broken, and the 'must' or grape juice comes in contact with the yeasts. Sometimes a special culture of yeast is added. Yeasts live and multiply by feeding on the sugar in the grape juice, transforming it into alcohol and carbon dioxide and forming numerous flavour compounds in the process.

Tannins, the strong, slightly bitter flavouring in red wines, come mainly from the grape's skin. (They are also found in tea.) During fermentation the alcohol formed extracts colour, tannin and other flavour pigments from the grape skins, and the colour of the fermenting wine deepens. When sufficient colour and tannin have been extracted, the liquid is drained off and the skins, pips and other solids are pressed to extract any remaining juice. This 'press wine' is more concentrated in colour, tannins and extract than the free-run juice, but may be rather harsh and rough in flavour. The two are often kept separate, although some or all of the press wine may be added back to the free-run wine to give colour, body and structure as required.

A little sulphur dioxide is often added to the grapes before the fermentation, to inhibit the action of bacteria and to allow the wine yeasts to start their work. The sulphur acts as a disinfectant and antioxidant, and also helps to extract colour from the grape skins. Red wines are generally fermented at a temperature of between 25°C and 30°C. Too cold, and the yeasts cannot work so efficiently; too hot, and the yeasts will be killed. If the must becomes too hot or too cold, the fermentation will 'stick', risking bacterial spoilage and oxidation.

The temperature of fermentation will affect the finished flavours of the wine. Colour extraction is more efficient at higher temperatures, but at high temperatures the fermentation will take place more quickly, and some of the flavour constituents of the grape may literally be boiled away. The wine will have less aroma, less colour, and a less fine flavour. Temperature rises during fermentation; the action of the yeasts rapidly increases the heat within the liquid by several degrees, and the wine-maker must keep a careful watch and chill the fermenting liquid if necessary. If the fermentation temperature is too low, the wine will have less colour, the flavour extracted from the skins will be less intense, and the wine may risk acquiring strong grassy, herbaceous aromas.

After all the grape sugar has been converted to alcohol, the yeasts have nothing left to feed on and die, falling to the bottom of the fermentation vessel. If the grapes were exceptionally high in sugar, the yeasts may be killed by the alcohol they have formed before all the sugar has been converted. This happens when the wine reaches around 15 per cent alcohol. Any remaining sugar will then remain in the wine as sweetness.

The process of fermentation generally lasts between ten days and two weeks, the majority of sugar being converted in the first few days, while the yeasts quickly multiply and reach their peak of production. The new wine froths and bubbles as carbon dioxide is produced, and at the end of the two weeks will still be slightly gassy. When the skins and pips are removed, the wine is placed in clean containers, where it will continue to fizz gently as the last of the gas escapes and the last of the sugar is converted by the yeasts. By the spring, most of the gas will have disappeared and the wine will have thrown a heavy sediment, composed of dead yeast cells and the particles left after pressing.

Malolactic Fermentation

The wine next undergoes malolactic fermentation, a bacterial process by which the malic acid (the acidity found in apples) is converted by bacteria into lactic acid (the acidity found in milk). This process is necessary for the stability of red wine, and gives a softer, rounder, more 'winey' and less 'grapey' flavour. It also produces more carbon dioxide gas, and the wine remains slightly fizzy until the process is complete.

Ageing

If the desired style is youthful and fruity, the wine will be ready for bottling as soon as it has finished its malolactic fermentation. The ultimate example of this is in the growing market for *vin nouveau*, or *vin primeur*, where the wine undergoes both fermentation and malolactic fermentation as quickly as possible, and is filtered, bottled and sold in October/November, only a couple of months after the grapes have left the vine.

The opposite phenomenon is where the wine is aged for a couple of years or longer in cask, to smooth and develop its flavours, and to permit a certain 'controlled oxidation', before it is bottled. Wine ages faster in bulk than in bottle, as it has more contact with the air. The larger the container, the smaller the percentage of wine in direct contact with the air and the slower the process of oxidation. In the same way, the more tightly sealed the tank, the more oxygen can be excluded and the slower the process of ageing. Thus, wine in a small oak barrel will age much more rapidly than wine in a large stainless steel tank.

Newly made wine will have certain smells left over from the fermentation; it may smell 'yeasty' or 'appley'. These smells will disappear naturally as the wine ages, to be replaced by much pleasanter 'winey' smells of fruit and spice. The wine will breathe much more readily in a small oak barrel than in a large stainless steel tank, and will make this transformation much more rapidly.

After maturation the wine is ready for bottling. Red wines may be filtered or fined. Generally, the cheaper the wine, the more filtering and fining it will have received, as sediment is less acceptable in a cheap wine than in a finer estate wine.

Macération Carbonique

This method of producing red wines is now widely used in Languedoc-Roussillon. Although it is considered a development of the twentieth century, variations of *macération carbonique* have been used in wine-making for hundreds of years. The technique was known as *vinification en grains entiers*, or whole grape vinification. The practice had almost disappeared at the beginning of this century, but has seen a great revival in more recent times. Whole uncrushed bunches of grapes are put into a vat, where the weight of the top bunches breaks the skins of grapes lower down the vat. The juice released by the lower bunches starts to ferment, releasing carbon dioxide gas. The vat is closed, retaining the carbon dioxide, which replaces the oxygen in the vat. The whole unbroken grapes start an intracellular fermentation in an atmosphere surrounded by carbon dioxide. Fermentation continues over eight to fifteen days at a temperature of around 30°C. When the desired colour and flavour have been reached, the grapes are pressed in the usual way and the wine can then finish its fermentation normally. *Macération carbonique* extracts colour without extracting the harsher tannins in the skins, giving a deep-coloured but soft-flavoured wine. It works well with tannic grape varieties such as Carignan, giving aroma and reducing astringency.

The only new, twentieth-century aspect of this process is the use of stainless steel vats, in which the fermenting grapes can be more hermetically sealed than in the old wooden vats.

Rosé Wine Vinification

Rosé wines are made from red-skinned grape varieties, but the skins are left with the fermenting juice for just a few hours, in order to extract only a small amount of their colouring matter. Rosé wines may vary in colour from the very palest 'blush' wines, sometimes designated *gris*, or even *gris de gris*, to a deep pink, almost light red colour, as with St-Saturnin's Vin d'une Nuit, in which the grape skins are removed after one night's fermentation. Sometimes red grapes are 'bled' to give better colour to a red wine; the first juice extracted is used to produce a rosé, leaving less juice to produce the red wine, a higher skin/juice ratio, and therefore a deeper-coloured, more concentrated red wine. A rosé produced in this way is sometimes called a *saignée*.

After the fermenting juice is separated from the skins, it is left to finish the fermentation, then usually bottled quite quickly, to preserve its youthful freshness. The fermentation is usually carried out at a cooler temperature than for a red wine – around 17-22°C – in order to preserve freshness and bouquet. The cooler the temperature, the more aromatic the wine will be; as the temperature of fermentation becomes warmer, the wine will be softer and fatter. Some rosé wines may be aged for a short time in wood, giving a softer, rounder, more mellow flavour, but most is kept as fresh and grapey as possible.

White Wine Vinification

White wines are usually produced from white grapes, but since, as we have seen, the juice of most grapes is colourless, it is also possible to produce white wines from red grape varieties. The juice is usually separated from the skins by crushing and pressing the grapes as soon as they arrive at the winery. As with rosé wine production, fermentation takes place at a cool temperature, generally between 17° and 22°.

White wines from this region were often criticized in the past for being flabby, over-alcoholic, and lacking in acidity. This can be counteracted by picking the grapes before they are fully ripe to preserve acidity and to limit sugar content, and by cool fermentation processing. Until earlier this century it was quite hard to control the temperature of fermentation. The outside temperature at picking time was often 25-30°C, and the grapes arrived at the winery at this temperature. The fermentation process itself causes heat, and the fermenting juice would therefore rise another few degrees. The only ways to cool the juice were to keep the cellar as cool as possible, with thick walls and roofs, and to soak the outsides of the tanks with cold water. Occasionally lumps of ice were even put into the fermenting liquid.

Modern techniques have altered white wine vinification beyond recognition over the last twenty years. Temperature control is now an exact science, and white wines can be vinified in clinically sterile surroundings to extract the maximum fruit flavours.

White wines do not always undergo malolactic fermentation; the wine may be filtered and kept cool enough to prevent malolactic fermentation from taking place. This will give a white wine more grapey fruit flavours and more freshness.

Usually must is separated from the grape skins as soon as possible in white wine production, but there is now more experimentation with *macération pelliculaire*, skin contact. The grape skins are left in contact with the fermenting must for up to twenty-four hours, to extract aromas and flavours from the skin. This is a delicate process, as the skins floating on the vats may attract bacterial spoilage, and a white wine is always far more vulnerable to spoilage than a red wine.

With modern vinification techniques there is no longer any reason why Languedoc-Roussillon should not produce top-quality white wines.

Rancio Wines

The term *rancio* may occasionally be met on a wine label. Taken literally, this would signify that the wine is 'rancid' or 'off'. There has always been a vogue for 'aged' wines in parts of Languedoc-Roussillon, and both fortified and unfortified wines may be deliberately left to age in cask until they acquire a slightly musty, bitter-toffee flavour that may be an acquired taste. It is much more common with fortified than unfortified wines, but is found occasionally in whites from the Clairette grape, for example.

Sparkling Wine Vinification

The only AOC sparkling wine from Languedoc-Roussillon is Blanquette de Limoux, although there are numerous other sparkling wines produced in the region without the benefit of the AOC. In common with all AOC sparkling wines in France, Blanquette de Limoux is made by the *méthode champenoise*. This is a somewhat sore point at present, the Champenoise having requested that other sparkling wines find an alternative name for their *méthode*. *Traditionelle* fits very well in the case of Blanquette de Limoux, whose sparkling wines have as long a history as Champagne. Benedictine monks were studying sparkling wine production in Limoux at around the time of Dom Pérignon's experiments in Champagne.

Sparkling wine is produced by retaining the natural carbon dioxide gas formed during fermentation. In normal wine production the gas bubbles off the fermenting must and is lost. Originally the gas was retained in a sparkling wine by bottling it midway through fermentation, which then finished off in the bottle, leaving some fizz, and a little sediment. This was unsatisfactory because of the sediment, and because it was hard to judge the degree of fizziness. Some bottles would have too little sparkle, other bottles would burst from too much.

Nowadays a still white wine is produced and is then bottled in a specially strengthened bottle, together with a carefully controlled dose of *vin de liqueur*, or sugared wine, and a specific type of yeast, adapted to work well in these conditions. The wine then undergoes a second fermentation in the bottle. The bottles are stacked horizontally, each row supported on wooden strips known as *lattes*. The sediment formed has then to be removed from the bottle, without losing too much of the sparkle. The bottles are placed on slanted wooden racks, known as *pupitres*, where the neck of each bottle is inserted in a specially designed hole and the bottles are gradually turned from a horizontal to a vertical upside-down position, gathering up the sediment in the process and moving it all into the neck of the bottle. The bottles are then entered, neck downwards, into a freezing solution. The small frozen lump of sediment may then be removed from the bottle, and a new cork inserted, without losing much of the sparkle.

This process produces the finest sparkling wines, with small, even bubbles of carbon dioxide which have been absorbed in the wine and which will continue to flow for many hours after the bottle has been opened. It is an expensive process, the sparkle being produced individually in each bottle.

Cheaper sparkling wine may be produced by a second fermentation in tank. Still white wine is put into a closed pressurized tank, together with yeasts and sugar, and the second fermentation takes place in the tank. The wine is then filtered from the sediment and bottled, still under pressure. Wines made by this method will have the words *vin mousseux* on the label. The sparkle does not generally last so well with this type of manufacture, which is not allowed for quality wine production.

Ageing Vessels Old and New

The way in which a wine has been aged will have an effect on its flavour. A wine that has been bottled soon after fermentation will be fresh and fruity, while a wine aged in cask will be softer and mellower in character. The size and material of the ageing vessel will also have some bearing on the character of the finished wine.

Stainless steel tanks have several important advantages: they are easy to clean, so that the risk of leaving bacteria or moulds that will contaminate the next batch of wines is eliminated. They are very long-lasting, and the temperature of the wine can be easily controlled by heating or cooling elements within the vat, while excessive air contact can be avoided by pumping nitrogen or carbon dioxide into the top of the vat to displace the oxygen. They can be custom-built, with the most sophisticated systems of automatic control, including readings of temperature, analysis of the sugar, alcohol, and other components of the wine controllable from a central panel, and they provide a very economic use of space in the winery. However, they are expensive, and because of the size often need to be assembled in a permanent position in the winery.

Some wineries, especially some of the older co-operatives, have cement wine vats. These are lined with glass tiles, or with a special epoxy resin lining, to prevent the concrete coming in contact with the wine and giving 'off' flavours. Concrete tanks are easy and cheap to install, and make efficient use of space, but are more liable to accidental damage than stainless steel. The lining has to be regularly checked for damage, and may have to be repaired every few years. These tanks are often hard to heat or cool down, and like stainless steel may cause the wine to retain 'off' flavours. Many of the tanks were sunk into the ground, giving ideal insulation, and the wine matures very slowly in these conditions, making them useful storage containers.

Wood is the traditional material for cask-building, and many of the older cellars still have wooden casks. These are less easy to clean, but are pleasing aesthetically. They have the advantage of a slightly rough surface, which helps the wine to throw tartrate deposits. They 'breathe', unlike stainless steel, helping the wine to lose any fermentation 'stink' and to develop aromas, and to age gracefully, with controlled oxidation. Old wooden casks do not impart oak flavours to the wine, although they might give a slightly 'woody' flavour that can be very attractive in moderation. The staves of the large casks are often 5-10 centimetres thick, and this provides a certain temperature control, insulating the wine from the outside temperature. They last very well, and many casks in use today are over 100 years old.

Small oak casks, such as are used in Bordeaux, are used in some cellars in Languedoc-Roussillon. These are becoming increasingly popular, and there is a brisk market in both new and second-hand casks. Small casks increase the wine's contact with the air, and therefore mature the wine much more rapidly. The newer the wood, the more strongly its flavour is imparted to the wine, and the wine-maker must be careful to ensure that the wine does not end up tasting of new wood rather than grapes. Oak-aged wine is definitely seen as a quality criterion at present. Oak is fashionable, and co-operatives, *négociants* and small domaines alike are producing a multitude of wines labelled variously *vinifié en barriques, fûts de chêne, élevé en barriques*. This gives the wine the 'boutique winery' handcrafted image that is popular with consumers both in France and abroad.

In the 1990 Concours tasting to choose the best and most typical wines of the Corbières district, fifteen out of the fifty-seven reds chosen had some mention of oak-ageing on the label. Oak can add to the complexity of the wine, adding a toasty spicy note to the fruit flavours, as long as it is not overdone. It gives the wine a softer, smoother flavour which makes it easier to drink in its youth. It adds several francs to the bottle price; the barrels are expensive, especially when purchased new, and when they have to be regularly replaced in order to impart the maximum flavour to the wine. The extra labour has to be taken into account. Each cask has to be regularly topped up and checked. Racking, or moving the wine off its sediment into a clean cask to prevent 'off' flavours, is much more labour-intensive with a number of small containers than with one or two large ones.

5

Grape Varieties

The grape variety or varieties from which a wine is made will influence the wine's flavour to a great extent. The smaller the yield, the more concentrated the grape flavour; the larger the yield, the more neutral the wine will appear. Even the world's finest varieties will not taste of much if yields are too big, while some of the more lowly regarded varieties are capable of producing very good-quality wines where yields have been limited. Many wines are produced from a blend of several varieties, and indeed many of the appellations stipulate a blend, but there are also an increasing number of varietal wines, those which state the grape variety used on the label. The following list is by no means exhaustive, but indicates the main varieties found in Languedoc-Roussillon.

Red Varieties

Red varieties have always been traditional in Languedoc-Roussillon, both for the production of table wines and for Vins Doux Naturels. Vinification techniques have changed less for reds than for whites, but nevertheless there is an increasing use of oak *barriques*, which can enhance the character of red varieties, softening the rougher tannic edges of harsher varieties and adding flavour to more neutral ones. Blending of several varieties has always been more traditional for reds than for whites, with each component of the blend contributing its own nuances to the whole. Most widely found is the trilogy of Carignan, Cinsault and Grenache, the staple red varieties of the entire Languedoc-Roussillon region. With the recent additions to the appellations of *cépages améliorateurs* such as Mourvèdre and Syrah, and small amounts of Cabernet Sauvignon and Merlot, many red wines in the region may have as many as seven or eight components in their blend.

There is also increasing interest in single varietal wines, sold as Vins de Pays. Most commonly found are Cabernet Sauvignon, Merlot, Syrah, Mourvèdre and Grenache, as well as blends of Cabernet and Merlot.

Alicante-Bouschet

COLOUR	Red
DISTRIBUTION	Widely grown, but for Vin de Table only

Not to be confused with the Alicante, a local name for Grenache, Alicante-Bouschet is a cross between Petit Bouschet (Teinturier du Cher × Aramon) and Grenache. A number of crosses were produced in the 1850s by Louis Bouschet, working near Montpellier, of which Alicante-Bouschet is the most widely cultivated and is the only 'recommended' Bouschet cross for wine-making in France. Alicante-Bouschet produces wine with a good deep colour, and for this reason it was always in demand by *négociants* for blending and fetched a higher price than most varieties in the last century. It is often used to produce grape juice, being a *teinturier* grape, one of the few with coloured juice.

In the first legislation on permitted varieties by the Institut des Vins de Consommation Courante, Alicante-Bouschet was listed as 'authorized', but not recommended, although there was pressure to have it upgraded, and indeed it eventually was. An early-budding and early-ripening variety, it is one of the first to be harvested in southern France, at the end of August or early September. It prefers fertile soil, is a high-yielding variety, and is generally spur-pruned to control yield. It has excellent resistance to fungal diseases. The foliage turns completely red in the autumn, and is very striking.

In a blend, it will add colour to the wine but does not have much flavour. Although it is gradually being replaced by better-quality varieties, there are still nearly 22,000 hectares of Alicante-Bouschet planted in Languedoc-Roussillon, mostly producing very undistinguished wines.

Aramon

COLOUR	Red
DISTRIBUTION	Widely grown, particularly in Languedoc

Aramon was widely planted in the last century but is now being slowly phased out. It was used to provide enormous yields of undistinguished and anonymous wine. Aramon is a very productive variety, especially when grown on fertile soil with sufficient water. As its colour is pale, it was often blended with *teinturier*, or coloured-juice varieties. These wines became less popular after the introduction of Algerian wines on to the French market in the 1950s, and plantings of Aramon have declined since then. Aramon needs a long growing season, budding early and ripening late. It has excellent resistance to fungal diseases, and is a very reliable cropper. It is generally *gobelet*-trained to control its vigour. In good sites it can produce a quite attractive fruity wine, but it does not have much class on the whole, and is being replaced by Grenache, Syrah and Mourvèdre in most regions.

Mas de Daumas Gassac had 5 hectares of very old Aramon vines when it was purchased by Aimé Guibert in the 1970s, but to his subsequent regret he had them removed. It would have been interesting to see what old Aramon vines would have produced on top-quality land with careful wine-making.

Aspiran

COLOUR	Red
DISTRIBUTION	Minervois, Costières, not widely grown
SYNONYM	Ribeyrenc

Aspiran is found only in a few vineyards in Minervois and Costières du Nîmes, but was much more widely planted in the last century, before it was decimated by oïdium. It is moderately productive, and produces well-coloured wine, with good balance, and quite good aroma, but it is not very hardy, succumbing easily to fungal diseases.

Cabernet Sauvignon

COLOUR	Red
DISTRIBUTION	Malepère, Aude, otherwise Vin de Pays only, quite widely grown

The ubiquitous Cabernet Sauvignon is gaining a foothold in many parts of Languedoc-Roussillon. It was traditionally planted in parts of Aude and Pyrénées-Orientales in the 1800s, but was largely abandoned when vines were re-planted after phylloxera. Although some appellations allow a percentage of Cabernet Sauvignon in the blend, many of the regions can grow it only if they forgo appellation status, which is a great shame, given the quality of the wine it can produce and the fact that it was planted in the region in the last century. It is almost as though growers in the most expensive and most prestigious vineyard regions of France have sought to 'copyright' certain varieties. Chardonnay has had the same blocking legislation applied to it. Large amounts of Cabernet have been planted since the late 1970s, with the advent of Vin de Pays legislation, allowing growers more freedom to choose from a range of varieties.

Professor Boobals of Montpellier University recommends the use of Cabernet throughout the region except in very hot, dry inirrigable areas. He also recommends its vinification by *macération carbonique*, as the wine can otherwise be very tannic. Cabernet Sauvignon produces very deep-coloured wine, high in tannin, with rich blackcurrant fruit and good acidity. It often requires long ageing, but gives backbone and ageing potential to wines from softer varieties. A wine from 100 per cent Cabernet Sauvignon can sometimes be rather hard, vegetal and tough, and care is needed in vinification. It can produce excellent wines in the cooler vineyard sites, where the yield has been limited, and although its character is less marked with higher yields, Cabernet still produces distinctive wine.

It is late to bud, and matures in mid-season. It cannot cope well with drought, but is generally a reliable producer and adapts well to a wide variety of soils. While it would be a mistake to abandon less fashionable varieties altogether in favour of the famous, and therefore easy to sell, Cabernet, it has a very definite role to play in Languedoc-Roussillon.

Cabernet Franc

COLOUR	Red
DISTRIBUTION	Malepère, Aude, a small amount for Vin de Pays

Cabernet Franc is often seen as the poor relation of Cabernet Sauvignon. The wines are a little lighter and more delicate in style, and the vines are more vigorous and ripen earlier. It is also less choosy as to soil conditions. Cabernet Franc is generally grown for blendings, usually in conjunction with Cabernet Sauvignon. It is found mainly in the Aude *département*.

Carignan

COLOUR	Red, a little white
DISTRIBUTION	Very widely planted throughout region
SYNONYM	Roussillonen, Catalan

Carignan is one of the most widely planted varieties in Languedoc-Roussillon, accounting for up to 90 per cent of the vineyard area in parts of Aude and Hérault. It is almost the only variety found in some communes, and was formerly planted across the whole of southern France, from Provence to the Pyrenees. Carignan is a vigorous grower, very adaptable to the different soil types and rootstocks and to the climatic variations throughout the region. It is a hardy variety, and its regular yield in all vintages gives the grower security. The grapes are thick-skinned and therefore resistant to most diseases, although this variety can be susceptible to oïdium and peronospera. Professor Boobals of Montpellier University recommends it in the hotter regions, but on poor soils only. Carignan plantations are decreasing as more fashionable varieties take over, and many very old vineyards are being T-budded or uprooted to make way for other varieties.

Wines from Carignan are best described as 'rustic'. They are high in alcohol, deep-coloured, full-bodied, tannic, and sometimes coarse when young, although they become supple and attractive after two to three years, and can develop a gamey, spicy, rich flavour. Carignan is not a very aromatic variety. In a blend, it gives the wine structure and body. On its own it can be somewhat hard, and is better de-stemmed or vinified by *macération carbonique* to offset its austerity. It is not generally vinified traditionally, unless the wine is for long ageing.

Although it can be found trained either in the traditional *gobelet* style or on wires, with one long cane, the *gobelet* training gives by far the better results, limiting the yield and curbing the natural vigour of the plant. It produces its best wines on thin stony or slaty soil, for the same reason. On rich fertile soil the yield can be well over 100 hectolitres per hectare. The best results are produced with a maximum yield of 45-50 hectolitres per hectare, and a wine of between 11.5° and 12° alcohol.

Because it is widely grown throughout the region, it can be taken for granted that many wines will contain a greater or lesser percentage of this variety within the blend. On the other hand, it is not a fashionable variety, so it is unlikely to be named on the main wine label, although it often appears in the small print on the back label. Some very fine wines are produced from Carignan, although the taste is less immediately appealing than that of Cabernet, for example. Domaine d'Aupilhac in Montpeyroux produces a superb Vin de Pays from very old vines, yielding around 45 hectolitres per hectare.

Many appellations stipulate a maximum percentage of Carignan within the blend, and it is sometimes used as a 'loophole' variety within a single vineyard both for Appellation Controlée wine, at a yield of around 45-50 hectolitres per hectare, and also for a Vin de Pays wine, at 80-90 hectolitres per hectare. This permits the unscrupulous grower to produce a large yield, using the maximum permitted for the AC, and the surplus for Vin de Pays, thus officially not over-producing. Although this was not the purpose when the Vin de Pays laws were produced, there is little the authorities can do to prevent the practice.

Carignan Blanc is not widely grown, but is found in parts of the Coteaux du Languedoc, where it produces average to very good white wines, depending on yield and vinification.

Cinsault

COLOUR	Red
DISTRIBUTION	Very widely grown
SYNONYM	Plante d'Arles

Cinsault probably originated in southern France. Very little is grown in Roussillon, but plenty in Languedoc and also in the Rhône Valley and in parts of Provence. Professor Boobals classes it as suitable for the same sites as Carignan. Until recently, Cinsault, together with Carignan and Grenache, formed the basic trilogy of varieties found ubiquitously throughout the Aude, Hérault and Gard departments. Many co-operatives throughout the region survive on a staple diet of these three varieties: Cinsault to give fruit and finesse, Carignan for body and weight, and Grenache for alcohol and fatness. Cinsault on its own can give an attractive wine of between 12° and 12.5° alcohol, with softness, finesse, subtlety and fruit when grown in poor soil and restricted in yield.

The branches of the Cinsault vine have a tendency to droop, hence its local name, 'Cinsault Couché'. It is a moderately vigorous variety, and its large oval fruits make good table grapes. It is also attractive to birds. Cinsault has a shorter vegetative cycle than most red varieties of the region, and although budbreak is late, it is one of the first to ripen, at the beginning of September. It is resistant to drought, heat and winds, and favours dry stony slopes. In wet weather it can suffer from mildew. When grown on rich fertile soils it tends to yield very large crops, and therefore to lose character. According to Galet, the acreage in France has almost doubled since 1958, as growers try to improve their wine quality.

Cinsault is an ideal variety for rosé wine production, and is often used for this.

Counoise

COLOUR	Red
DISTRIBUTION	Collioure, Costières, Coteaux du Languedoc, Cabardès
SYNONYM	Aubun, Moustardier

Counoise is found in parts of the southern Rhône and Provence, and also in Languedoc-Roussillon. Professor Boobals cites it as recommended in all soils in the warmest areas of Languedoc, and for rosé wine production in cooler vineyards.

Counoise is a late budding and ripening variety, only moderately productive, and with good resistance to fungal diseases. It gives a wine that is attractively spicy and full-flavoured, with quite good alcohol content and moderate colour, for medium term ageing. It is usually planted in conjunction with other varieties, to provide elegance and flavour in a blend.

Fer

COLOUR	Red
DISTRIBUTION	Cabardès region only
SYNONYM	Fer Servadou

Fer is the principal grape variety in Marcillac, in south-west France. It also enters into blends in parts of Aude. Originally from the Bergerac area, Fer produces a light elegant wine, moderately coloured, with moderate alcohol and quite a strong distinctive bouquet. It can give softness and elegance to a blend.

Grenache Rouge/Gris/Blanc

COLOUR	Red, white and *gris*
DISTRIBUTION	Very widely grown throughout region
SYNONYM	Alicante

The Grenache probably originates from Spain, where it is known as the Garnacha or Granatxa. Grenache, also referred to as Gernache or Vernache, started to appear in the region as early as the mid 1300s. It was, and still is, used to produce the red Vins Doux Naturels in Banyuls, Maury and Rivesaltes. It is also used as part of the famous trilogy with Carignan and Cinsault, to give alcohol, fatness and generosity. The traditional planting for table wine was often two-thirds Carignan and one-third Grenache Noir. Grenache is less productive than Carignan. Until the last century Grenache Noir was the only colour grown, but during this century there has been an expansion in the planting of Grenache Gris and Grenache Blanc, both of which are less liable to suffer from poor flower set (*coulure*) than the Noir.

Grenache Noir likes a poor, dry arid soil with low organic matter, where it can produce rich, full-flavoured wines, high in natural alcohol. On rich fertile soils it often lacks character. Professor Boobals recommends Grenache in most of the region, but only in poor soils in the cooler districts. Some research is being done to select stocks against *coulure*. It is an otherwise vigorous vine, resistant to drought and to oïdium, although sensitive to powdery mildew. It is generally trained in *gobelet* style.

Grenache Noir produces wines with a deep colour, which can have up to 17° or 18° natural potential alcohol. This makes it ideal for Vins Doux Naturels. The wines often have low acidity, and are generally very fruity when young, with raspberry and blackcurrant flavours. This flavour changes to cherry and plum with maturity, when the wines can have a tendency to brown in colour and to dry out. Grenache is generally quite low in tannin, and supple, which makes it excellent in a blend with more tannic varieties such as Carignan, Syrah, Cinsault and Mourvèdre. The wines can lack the extract to back up the alcohol, although the best Vins Doux Naturels last and improve for many years.

Because of its difficulties with *coulure*, Grenache Noir now accounts for only around 20 per cent of the Grenache grown in Languedoc-Roussillon, and 11 per cent of that grown in Roussillon. Its main areas are around Maury and Banyuls. Grenache Gris became fashionable in the 1950s. It is more productive, and makes wine high in alcohol. Grenache Blanc accounts for over 20 per cent of the plantations of Roussillon. It produces wines lower in alcohol, and less fine in flavour. The white and *gris* varieties are used mainly for Vins Doux Naturels production, and not often for table wines, as they lack acidity unless blended with other varieties.

Lladoner Pelut

COLOUR	Red
DISTRIBUTION	Coteaux du Languedoc, Faugères, Minervois, Côtes du Roussillon
SYNONYM	Grenache Velu

There is some controversy over this variety: some experts consider that it is almost identical to the Grenache Noir, and is a mutation, others that it is a separate variety, although a close relative of Grenache. The two are identical in most characteristics, the main difference being in the appearance of the undersides of the leaves, which in the Lladoner Pelut are hairy, almost velvety, at some stages of growth, leading to its other name of Grenache Velu (Velvety Grenache). The true Grenache Noir has smooth leaves. Lladoner Pelut is less liable to *coulure*, and generally produces a less alcoholic wine. For this reason it is forbidden for Vins Doux Naturels.

Malbec

COLOUR	Red
DISTRIBUTION	Cabardès, Malepère, not widely planted
SYNONYM	Cot

Malbec is grown in parts of the Pyrénées-Orientales and sometimes in Languedoc to soften wines made from the harsher Carignan. Budbreak and maturity are early, and Malbec is moderately vigorous. While less aromatic than Cabernet, it is softer and more forward, with good colour and body.

Merlot

COLOUR	Red
DISTRIBUTION	Malepère, parts of Aude, also increasingly for Vin de Pays

Professor Boobals recommends Merlot in the coolest parts of the Languedoc, except for north-facing sites, where it risks *coulure*. It is not recommended in hotter vineyards, especially in dry inirrigable sites. Merlot is more productive than Cabernet, and is inceasing in popularity. It has been grown in parts of the Pyrénées-Orientales for many years, and is now found more widely throughout Languedoc-Roussillon for Vin de Pays production. It is classified as a recommended variety, and is popular because it ripens sooner than many local varieties, and gives a supple, well-coloured wine of good quality which is ready to drink when young and does not require long ageing. Merlot is a vigorous, productive variety, which buds early and ripens comparatively early in southern France. On its own, it produces wines that are attractive but rarely very fine. In conjunction with other grapes, it can produce excellent-quality wines.

Mourvèdre

COLOUR	Red
DISTRIBUTION	Increasing in popularity throughout the region
SYNONYM	Mataro, Espar

The Mourvèdre variety was widely planted throughout the Mediterranean region in the last century, and has been planted in southern France since at least the sixteenth century. It is less widely found today, although its use is increasing, as a recommended *cépage améliorateur*. Mourvèdre is originally from Spain, and is the main grape variety in Bandol in Provence. It was praised by Dr Guyot in the 1860s, in his opinion a very precious variety to give solid, honest and unchanging wine. Mourvèdre produces spicy, almost gamey wines, with a very deep opaque colour when young, rich in dry extract and tannin, full-bodied and with good alcohol. The wines can be closed and harsh when young, but develop well and can be very long-lived. Mourvèdre is excellent blended with Grenache, when it retards the Grenache's tendency to oxidation and produces a well-balanced wine with plenty of aroma and flavour.

Mourvèdre has some of the same characteristics as Carignan in the vineyard, but produces a small and very variable yield. It is a late-budding variety, which means that it generally avoids damage by spring frosts, and also avoids the risk of *coulure*. It matures late, necessitating a warm vineyard. It is long-lived and resistant to rot. It does not marry well with some rootstocks, especially those based on *riparia*, which were widely used after phylloxera. For these reasons it is not always popular with vine-growers. New clonal selection has greatly improved the regularity of yields, but the problem now is to get growers to forget its reputation as a hard-to-grow variety.

There is very little Mourvèdre in Roussillon, although its use is growing. Plantations in Hérault and Gard are also increasing. Traditionally Mourvèdre was grown around the commune of St-Gilles in Gard, and growers in the Costières and in the Coteaux du Languedoc are slowly being re-converted to its qualities.

Négrette

COLOUR	Red
DISTRIBUTION	Cabardès, not widely planted

Négrette is grown in the Frontonnais region of France, and only in limited quantities around Cabardès in Languedoc. It has some of the characteristics of Malbec, and gives a good-quality wine, with supple ripe young fruit, a good bouquet and colour, but rather low acidity. For this reason it needs to be blended with other varieties. It is a different variety from the Négrette de Nice.

Oeillade

COLOUR	Red
DISTRIBUTION	Cabrières, otherwise quite rare

Oeillade is found only in small pockets in parts of Languedoc. It has similar characteristics to Cinsault, and is sometimes confused with the latter. It gives attractive, elegant, fruity wines, and adds softness and elegance in a blend. It was grown much more widely throughout the region until the last century. There is also a white variety.

Pinot Noir

COLOUR	Red
DISTRIBUTION	Growing in popularity for Vin de Pays production

Pinot Noir is an early-ripening variety, and as such basically unsuitable in Languedoc-Roussillon, except in the very coolest sites. It is, however, a variety that is well known to the consumer, and is growing in popularity throughout the newer wine regions of the world. Since the 1970s it has been planted in a wide range of vineyard sites in Languedoc-Roussillon, and is considered trendy. It works quite well as part of a blend in the Aude region, although it is difficult to see exactly what it contributes to the blend. In Languedoc, a number of the newer growers and some of the larger companies specializing in varietal wines are showing interest in Pinot Noir, producing it as a single variety. At best, it has a touch of the soft raspberry vegetal fruit reminiscent of Burgundy, but generally, it needs a good imagination to discern the varietal character.

Syrah

COLOUR	Red
DISTRIBUTION	Widely planted throughout the region

Syrah has been cultivated in France since Roman times, and originally came from the Far East. However, it has been widely grown in Languedoc-Roussillon only over the last few decades.

Syrah produces a wine with intense aromas of violets, spices, green pepper and tar. Its distinctive bouquet can overpower other varieties in a blend. The wine frequently has a deep opaque colour, and is resistant to oxidation. Often closed when young, Syrah can age extremely well, and needs several years to develop its full bouquet and flavour. Although firm and tannic when produced with small yields, it is less intensely flavoured with larger yields.

Syrah has to be cane-pruned to produce a good yield, as its basal buds are generally infertile. Both the Petite Syrah and the Grosse Syrah are found, the former being less fertile and vigorous but producing finer wine. It is a late-budding variety but produces excellent results in the cooler regions of Languedoc-Roussillon. It is very sensitive to drought, and has to be sheltered from strong winds. It has been widely planted in recent times, as a *cépage améliorateur*, to bring more aroma and finesse to a blend. Professor Boobals recommends its use on all infertile soils, but only when pruned to give moderate yields in hotter zones.

Tempranillo

COLOUR	Red
DISTRIBUTION	About 600 hectares in the Languedoc

Tempranillo is a Spanish variety found in parts of Languedoc-Roussillon. Professor Boobals recommends it for poorer soils in the cooler vineyard sites, and for warmer zones when vinified by *macération carbonique*. There were experimental plantings throughout the region in the 1970s, when it was intended to replace Carignan, but its lack of acidity is a problem, and the wine tends to lack character.

White Varieties

Red grape varieties are generally more successful in warmer vineyard sites, as the whites tend to ripen too quickly, losing the aromatic components in the grape and becoming flabby and lacking in acidity. The demand for chilled wine to accompany the seafood found along the Mediterranean coast has long been met by rosé wines, both in Provence and Languedoc-Roussillon, but there has been increasing consumer demand for white wines. Some red varieties have been vinified as whites, and some as *gris de gris*, the best known being Listel from Salins du Midi. With modern vinification techniques, and improved methods of viticulture, there has been enormous growth in white wine production in this region.

Growers are busy planting the fashionable white grapes of the moment: Chardonnay in particular is becoming commonplace, and Sauvignon is also increasing in popularity. The traditional white varieties of the region are also being revamped. By picking the grapes before they are fully ripe, a 'green' wine can be produced, with an attractive crisp acidity, lower alcohol, and an almost bitter flavour that is attractive when the wine is young. Cool fermentation temperatures retain the maximum fruit aromas, and the wine is not allowed to undergo malolactic fermentation, thereby keeping even more of its grape acidity. By retaining a small amount of carbon dioxide from the fermentation, this freshness can be further accentuated. These fresh, crisp wines need to be consumed in their youth, but there are also styles that age quite well.

Producers are experimenting with oak-ageing of white wines.
Chardonnay is particularly successful, but this technique can also be used to enhance otherwise quite bland varieties such as Picpoul. Varieties such as Viognier and Chardonnay can be picked fully ripe, and given a slight 'lift' by blending with varieties of higher natural acidity such as Chenin Blanc or Gros Manseng.

Bourboulenc

COLOUR	White
DISTRIBUTION	Small plantings throughout the region
SYNONYM	Tourbat, Vermentino

Bourboulenc was quite widely planted until the end of the last century, but is now being replaced by other varieties. It is usually blended, and can produce a thin, bland, anonymous wine if picked when just ripe, although it is capable of producing a powerful, rustic, full-flavoured, rich wine if picked late in the season, when the grapes are over-ripe.

Chardonnay

COLOUR	White
DISTRIBUTION	Blanquette de Limoux, widely grown for Vin de Pays

Chardonnay, 'the Gucci grape', has great cachet the world over. It has become almost a brand name, and consumers will buy practically any wine with the magical word Chardonnay on the label.

Chardonnay is a vigorous grower and an early ripener, often ripening in August in Languedoc-Roussillon. Because of the shorter growing season in warmer vineyard sites, the wines may lose some of the fragrant aromatic qualities for which Chardonnay is so justly famous in cooler regions such as Champagne and Chablis, but it is an easily pleased variety, and will perform equally well on hot, fertile, irrigated plain vineyards and on hillside vineyards with poor thin soil and smaller yields. The grape's main problem is that it loses acidity if picked over-ripe, and becomes rather flabby and alcoholic. For this reason the grower has to calculate the optimum picking date with care.

Because Chardonnay wines are in such demand, growers receive a premium for Chardonnay over any other variety grown, and many are planting and re-grafting as fast as vines can be made available. New wave producers in particular are paying high premiums to growers who are willing to turn over part or all of their vineyards to Chardonnay production.

Between the agricultural censuses of 1968 and 1979, Chardonnay rose from eleventh to fourth most important white grape variety in France, and plantations are still increasing at a tremendous rate.

Chardonnay produces wines that are high in alcohol and often in colour, with a light but not very pronounced lemon and fruit salad nose, and rich, broad, buttery fruit flavours. As long as the grapes are picked before over-maturity, the wines will age well and have good body and structure, especially where the yield is limited.

Chardonnay is often vinified in oak, which complements its flavours particularly well, and Languedoc-Roussillon is now buying oak in a big way, mainly for Chardonnay production but also increasingly for red wine production.

Improvements in wine-making technology, and large financial investments in modern wine-making cellars with temperature-controlled fermentation tanks and arrays of new oak barrels, are producing some very high-quality wines from the Chardonnay grape, although there are also many very neutral and bland wines hiding behind this label.

Chenin Blanc

COLOUR	White
DISTRIBUTION	Blanquette de Limoux, Coteaux du Languedoc, quite widely planted

Chenin Blanc has been grown in the Loire Valley since the ninth century, and has appeared in Languedoc-Roussillon in small quantities for the last couple of centuries. It is useful in providing freshness and acidity in white wine blends. Its vigour and productivity depend on vineyard conditions, and it can be pruned to produce large yields of bland wine, or more severely to produce sappy, crisp wine with a good balance of acidity. It is used as part of the blend in Blanquette de Limoux to give finesse and acidity.

Listel are producing some very good Chenin Blanc, and growers in the Coteaux du Languedoc are also making excellent wines with this variety.

Clairette Blanche/Rose

COLOUR	White, some *gris*
DISTRIBUTION	Widely distributed throughout region

Clairette is probably the oldest white variety of Languedoc-Roussillon, and has been grown here for many centuries. It is particularly suited to unfertile soils, where the yield can be limited. It is grown throughout the region, especially for the appellations Clairette du Languedoc and Clairette de Bellegarde. It is also used for the production of Vins Doux Naturels, and for vermouth production.

Clairette is a late ripener. It has upright branches, and medium-sized bunches of white grapes with a firm, fleshy texture. It makes a good table grape. Clairette wine is generally high in alcohol, with a pronounced bouquet. It is often blended with other varieties to give body and bouquet. It tends to oxidize rapidly, but this characteristic can be turned to advantage in the production of *rancio* wines, as for the appellation Clairette de Languedoc.

There is also a small amount of Clairette Rose, with pink-skinned grapes, otherwise identical to the white in flavour and character.

Maccabéo

COLOUR	White
DISTRIBUTION	Widely distributed throughout region

The Maccabéo or Maccabéu variety originated in the Spanish province of Catalonia, where it is widely used for *cava* sparkling wine production. It is used for Vins Doux Naturels production in the Agly Valley, and also for dry table wine production, especially in the Côtes du Roussillon.

Maccabéo is a vigorous variety, which must be planted in poor soils in order to limit yields. It suffers from drought, and is sensitive to winds, so vineyard sites need to be sheltered, in areas of reasonable rainfall.

Maccabéo produces wines of high alcohol (13-14°, or more) and low acidity, with good fruit and finesse. Its wines can be heavy and rather fat. Maccabéo is often picked slightly 'green', at 11-11.5°, to retain acidity and freshness. The picking date can be hard to judge, as the grapes gain richness very quickly during the last week or two of ripening. It is quite a skill to estimate the optimum vintage date. Maccabéo grapes are generally brought to the press as unbroken bunches, as they have to be very carefully vinified to avoid oxidation. This is often stipulated as part of the appellation.

Maccabéo produces excellent Vins Doux Naturels when picked fully ripe. The wines have a honeyed richness and ripeness. It can also be used to give body and roundness to red wines. Up to 10 per cent is used in many blends, which is sufficient to give the wines body without diluting their colour.

Malvoisie

COLOUR	White
DISTRIBUTION	Roussillon, very small plantations

The name Malvoisie can be very misleading, as it is sometimes used to denote the Bourboulenc, and is used in the Loire to denote Pinot Gris. The genuine Malvoisie has probably all but disappeared from France, although some growers in Roussillon claim to have small plantations of the real thing.

Malvoisie appeared in the Roussillon region in the mid 1300s, having been imported from Greece to produce sweet fortified wines of the style very popular at that date, which previously had only been produced in Cyprus and Greece. It was grown in Roussillon with apparent success, producing some of their very best Vins Doux Naturels. It produced highly scented wines, with deep golden colour and powerful fruit flavours, which had a great reputation for their ageing capacity.

Marsanne

COLOUR	White
DISTRIBUTION	Parts of Minervois, growing in popularity

Marsanne, one of the grape varieties grown for white Hermitage, is planted in the Rhône Valley and increasingly in Languedoc over the past few years. It is still fairly experimental in Languedoc, and is generally blended with other varieties to give body, weight, and a certain perfume to the blend. It has the potential to produce richly flavoured aromatic whites with very good ageing ability.

Mauzac

COLOUR	White
DISTRIBUTION	Blanquette de Limoux, Aude
SYNONYM	Blanquette

Mauzac is the grape variety used for the production of Blanquette de Limoux, the name Blanquette coming from the whitish colour of the undersides of the vine leaves. It probably originated in the Gaillac region. Mauzac wines are precocious, quick to show their character, and rapid to mature. The wines have a fine bouquet, slightly appley flavours, and an attractive hint of bitterness, with good acidity.

Muscat

COLOUR	White
DISTRIBUTION	Quite widely distributed, especially for Vins Doux Naturels
SYNONYM	Petits Grains = Frontignan
	Alexandrie = Romaine

There are many varieties of Muscat in the world today. The two varieties used in Languedoc-Roussillon are Muscat d'Alexandrie and Muscat à Petits Grains.

Muscat d'Alexandrie is also known as Zibbibo in Italy, and as White Hanepoot in South Africa. It is a popular table grape, but is slightly less aromatic than Muscat à Petits Grains. As it ripens late, it needs a very hot area, and Roussillon is the only part of France well suited to its needs. Muscat d'Alexandrie has been cultivated here since the nineteenth century, although Muscat à Petits Grains has a much longer history. Muscat d'Alexandrie is more resistant to drought, although its wine has less finesse. It ages well, giving raisiny, figgy flavours when mature. Because of the difficulty in obtaining a natural minimum of 14° with high yields in rich soils, legislation now states that new plantations must be of Muscat à Petits Grains, unless this already constitutes at least half of the total planted for any particular grower.

Muscat à Petits Grains is also known as Muscat de Frontignan. This is the variety used for Clairette de Die, and one of the varieties found in Alsace. It ripens earlier than Muscat d'Alexandrie, ripening from the beginning of September in warmer regions. It is, however, very popular with birds, wasps and bees. The Roman name for this vine, *Vitis apianae*, 'the bee vine', attests to this, and also to the wine's honeyed flavour. Muscat à Petits Grains can suffer from virus diseases, giving low yields and poor grape set, but improvements are being made with new clones. It likes a deep soil, not too dry or arid.

Muscat is mainly grown for production of white Vins Doux Naturels, for which only the two varieties described may be used. Sweet Muscat wines from Languedoc-Roussillon have been highly regarded for several centuries, and have their own appellations and regulations for the different regions. Muscat is mentioned in the 1600s, as one of the best wines of Rivesaltes and of Frontignan. There is also a small quantity of Muscat *vin de liqueur*, mainly from the Frontignan region, and a small but growing amount of dry white table wine from the Muscat grape.

Picardin

COLOUR	White
DISTRIBUTION	Rare, small amount still grown in Hérault

Picardin is found in small quantities, mainly in the Hérault region. It is also found in small amounts in the southern Rhône.

Picardin is a variety of the past. Jullien mentions that it was grown around the communes of Marseillan and Pomerols, near Béziers. He describes the wine as *liquoreux*, although unlike Muscat. The flavour was good, with good body, bouquet and alcohol, and the wine kept well and could even withstand long journeys without altering its character. It was often blended with other white varieties to give sweetness and strength, and some was made into *eau-de-vie*. Apparently the wine lost sweetness with age, became dry, and 'shared some of the flavour characteristics with the wines of the same type that we purchase at vast price from Spain', although Jullien stated that it did not have the finesse or perfume of the Spanish wines. Nowadays it is found in parts of Hérault, and is generally grown to be part of a blend.

Picpoul Blanc/Noir

COLOUR	White, red
DISTRIBUTION	Cabardès (red), Corbières (red and white), Pinet
SYNONYM	Piquepoul, Languedocien

Picpoul was widely grown in the Limoux region in the last century, but has gradually been replaced by Mauzac. It is the variety used in the production of the appellation Picpoul de Pinet, where modern cool fermentation techniques are producing some clean, attractive, if sometimes neutral wines. It is a late-budding and quite late-ripening variety, which can produce rather flabby wines unless picked at the right moment and carefully vinified. Picpoul is often blended with Clairette and Terret.

The red is usually blended with other varieties, and is hard to find on its own.

The name Picpoul is sometimes given to Folle Blanche, but the varieties are unrelated. There is also a small amount of Picpoul Gris in Languedoc.

Rolle

COLOUR	White
DISTRIBUTION	Coteaux du Languedoc, small but growing planting

Rolle was almost exclusively grown in Bellet, near Nice, until the last decade. It is now being grown very successfully in some of the hillside vineyards of Languedoc, where it has recently been added to the 'recommended' list of varieties. Some growers see it as a variety with good potential for the region. It produces quite alcoholic wines, but with good flavour and aroma. It is also a good table grape variety.

Roussanne

COLOUR	White
DISTRIBUTION	Parts of Minervois, not widely planted

Roussanne is found in the northern Rhône and Provence, and also in parts of Minervois. It is a late-ripening variety, giving a wine with great finesse and with a pronounced bouquet. It needs a hot vineyard site to ripen fully. Like Marsanne, it is increasing in popularity both for blending and for varietal wines.

Sauvignon Blanc

COLOUR	White
DISTRIBUTION	Rapidly increasing, especially in Languedoc

Sauvignon is a vigorous variety which matures early in southern France. It is increasing in popularity in Languedoc-Roussillon. When planted in a suitable site with limited yield, and fermented at a cool temperature, it can produce very attractive dry white wine, retaining good acidity and with a characteristic ripe gooseberry fruit flavour.

Sauvignon produces some excellent Vins de Pays, notably those from Guy & Peyre in the Coteaux de Murviel, and from Listel in the Golfe du Lion.

Terret Gris/Blanc/Noir

COLOUR	White, red and *gris*
DISTRIBUTION	Corbières, widely distributed

The Terret variety is found in Noir, Blanc, and Gris; the Gris, or Terret-Bourret, being the most widely planted in Languedoc-Roussillon, although the Blanc is also grown in large quantities. The Noir is much less widely found. Terret is occasionally found with all three colours of grape on one vine. The variety was introduced to the region in the 1800s. Dr Guyot, writing in the 1860s, condemned the wine from Terret as being uninteresting; before phylloxera it was widely used for distillation, and was the base for Languedoc's famous *eaux-de-vie*. More recently, much of the wine has been used in vermouth production.

Terret is a late-budding, vigorous variety, producing high yields, but ripening quite late, and therefore suited to warmer regions. The wine is fresh, clean, light, but without any great character. Terret is often picked before full ripeness, to retain acidity and freshness. Whites from the Blanc or Gris can be attractive in their youth, but do not have much ageing ability.

Ugni Blanc

COLOUR	White
DISTRIBUTION	Costières du Gard, Languedoc, quite widely planted

Ugni Blanc is recommended in the Languedoc-Roussillon region for dry white wine production. Of Italian origin, Ugni manages to retain its acidity even in moderately warm vineyards in southern France. It needs a warm climate to ripen, budding and ripening comparatively late, and is very vigorous, giving very large yields if unchecked. Its wines are generally undistinguished and neutral, but it is capable of producing excellent-quality wine if yields are carefully controlled. A late-picked Ugni produced by Domaine de Ravanès is outstanding.

Viognier

COLOUR	White
DISTRIBUTION	Very small plantations, increasing in popularity

Although Viognier is not permitted for appellation wines within Languedoc, it is growing in popularity for Vin de Pays production. The grape variety of Condrieu and Château Grillet in the northern Rhône, it has a unique perfume and flavour, and is being tried in many New World areas including California and Australia, as well as in parts of Languedoc. Viognier is a capricious variety, giving small yields, and it takes several years from planting until full production is reached. Growers in the hillside vineyards of Languedoc produce excellent wines from Viognier, and now some of the 'big boys' are starting to plant it in less propitious sites, seeing it as the fashionable grape of the future. Time will tell whether the quality will be sufficient to justify the low yields, and whether there will still be sufficient varietal flavour if higher yields are achieved.

Viognier certainly deserves to become more fashionable.

6

The Wine Regions

Quality Designations

The laws of Appellation Contrôlée in all parts of France specify that wines must be produced according to '*usages locaux, loyaux et constants*'; in other words, by traditional methods that have been handed down through the generations in each viticultural region. This is much harder to specify in Languedoc-Roussillon than in other parts of France, as so much has changed over the last century, and so much is in the process of changing at the present time.

Appellation Contrôlée (AC), or controlled naming, was a system set up in France to safeguard the quality of the best French wines. The system was set up under the Institut Nationale des Appellations d'Origine, the INAO. The precise boundaries within which each wine could be produced were defined, as were the grape varieties that could be grown and the style of wine that could be produced. Maximum yields and minimum alcohol content in the finished wine were also stipulated, in order to prevent over-production and the subsequent dilution of the wine. Originally only the very top vineyards received the accolade, as their growers were generally the most organized and were able to satisfy the authorities that wine production in their vineyard area was already well under control. Those wine areas which were less well organized were either turned down by the committee or given the intermediate status Vins Delimités de Qualité Supérieure (VDQS). This was seen either as a state of purgatory, while the region became more organized and prepared to upgrade to AC, or as a category for wines that were not quite good enough for the full accolade – 'good but simple country wines'.

Wines that were unable to attain either AC or VDQS status were unable to state their origins, and formed the great anonymous sea of 'plonk', or Vin de Table. If a French wine label states simply 'Vin de Table', this will denote the lowest-quality category in France, a wine without any 'pedigree'. These wines are also known as Vins de Consommation Courante, or VCC.

In 1979 a new category was introduced: Vins de Pays, or the 'élite of the Vins de Table'. This category bridged the gap between VDQS and VCC to some extent, allowing a regional and quality designation for wines otherwise outside the AC system. Unlike plain Vins de Table, a wine with Vin de Pays status can mention the region of origin, as well as the variety, the name of the domaine, and the vintage, if the producer wishes.

The quality control system has helped to stamp out many fraudulent practices, but has also come in for some criticism. Permitted grape varieties which have been specified for some regions were those grown at the moment of classification, and in southern France, where vineyards have been in a state of change for much of this century, many good, traditional varieties in use in the last century were excluded while less good but more productive varieties introduced at the beginning of the current century were laid down as the 'traditional grapes' of the region. Growers wishing to plant grape varieties not permitted under the AC laws are now increasingly turning to the Vins de Pays label.

The VDQS label is seen as rather ambiguous; wines in this category are often subject to even more constraints than they would be as AC, and with less benefits. Until 1980 VDQS wine statistics were included with those of Vins de Table, rather than with AC wines, and the consumer was and still is often unaware of the significance of VDQS. Until 1985, when all but two Languedoc-Roussillon regions were finally upgraded from VDQS to AC, Languedoc accounted for some 85 per cent of French VDQS production, with the constraints of yield, varieties, alcohol, organoleptic and chemical analysis and zone delimitation, but without the benefits of a true quality image.

Blanquette de Limoux, AOC

Factfinder	
STATUS	AOC
COLOUR	White
SIZE OF REGION	1,600 hectares
AVERAGE ANNUAL PRODUCTION	50,500 hectolitres
MAXIMUM YIELD	50 hectolitres per hectare
MINIMUM ALCOHOL	10°
MAXIMUM ALCOHOL	13°
STYLE	Sparkling, dry to medium

Grape Varieties	
MAUZAC	minimum 70 per cent
CHARDONNAY	maximum 20 per cent*
CHENIN BLANC	maximum 20 per cent*
	*(to a maximum 30 per cent combined)

Blanquette de Limoux is the only AOC sparkling wine produced in Languedoc-Roussillon. Most of the region is too warm to produce a wine with the necessary delicacy and acidity to make an attractive sparkling wine, but the altitude around Limoux is a mitigating factor, and the area has a long tradition of sparkling wine production. Blanquette has been famous throughout Europe since the sixteenth century, and was very popular in Paris taverns in the eighteenth century. The Limoux area is one of transitional climate; the Aquitaine climate to the west and the Montagnarde to the south moderate the heat and dryness of the Mediterranean zone. Thin topsoils of calcareous marl provide good drainage, while surface stones retain the heat during the day and reflect it at night.

Blanquette is made mainly from the Mauzac grape, which is known as Blanquette on account of the white downy appearance of the undersides of the vine leaves. The wine was originally made from Mauzac and Clairette, but since 1978 Chardonnay and/or Chenin Blanc are permitted as part of the blend, and can add finesse and acidity.

The maximum weight of grapes per hectare is also controlled, at 7,500 kilos, to give a maximum of 100 litres of juice per 150 kilos of grapes and to ensure that only the best juice, that which flows first when the grapes are pressed, is used. The bunches of grapes must be brought to the press whole and uncrushed. The wine must be made by the *méthode champenoise*, by secondary fermentation in the bottle. The secondary fermentation must be followed by a minimum of nine months on the lees, and the finished wine must be between 10° and 13° alcohol. The wine can be *brut*, *demi-sec* or *doux*, according to the dosage used.

Vin de Blanquette is a similar sparkling wine from this region, seldom seen in its traditional form, although the name may be used for the *méthode champenoise*. The traditional production was by the *méthode rurale*, using the natural grape sugar still present in the wine when bottled mid-way through the fermentation. This method leaves a light deposit in the bottle and gives an uneven amount of *mousse* and sweetness. Only a small proportion of Blanquette, around 1,500 hectolitres, is produced in this way. There is also a still wine produced in the region, called simply Limoux, or Vin de Limoux. This is from the same varieties, and production is only about 50 hectolitres per year.

The appellation is restricted to forty-two communes around Limoux, to the west of the Aude *département*. In 1929 growers formed the Syndicat de Défense du Cru

Blanquette de Limoux, to protect and promote the quality image. The *syndicat*, composed of a board of growers and producers, controls the picking date, monitoring grape maturation towards vintage time.

Production and sales are on the increase, due mainly to the efforts of the two Caves Coopératives, who have put a lot of effort into marketing the wines of this region. Production is coming up to around 7 million bottles a year, having increased over 115 per cent since the 1970s. In 1948 there were only 486 growers. Now there are over 1,000, as well as two co-operatives, and seven *élaborateurs*, who buy 17 per cent of the grapes produced, as well as 8 per cent of the wine produced by the growers. The co-operatives account for some 75 per cent of the entire production.

I must confess that this is not one of my favourite sparkling wines. All too often the wine is rather dull and lacking in character, but a well-made example can be attractive as an aperitif. Blanquette de Limoux should have a floral, sometimes slightly almondy acacia fragrance on the bouquet, and a freshness and vivacity on the palate, often with a slight, rather pleasant, bitterness on the finish. Many of the wines are vintage-dated, and most will be at their best between three and five years old, although some of the better wines will age well for up to eight or ten years, taking on a buttery, smoky, mellow flavour. (As with old champagne, this is probably an English taste.)

Expect to pay between 30 and 50 francs a bottle at the cellar door. There are not many really expensive de-luxe *cuvées*, although most producers seem to have two or more styles, the better *cuvée* generally a few francs more expensive than the other wines.

Co-opérative Aimery (650 members) produces several *cuvées* – Aldéric Brut, Sieur d'Arques, Prestige d'Aimery. The Prestige is produced only in good vintages, and is toastier and spicier in style, very well made, and one of the best wines produced in the region.

Château d'Antugnac, Marc Ramires – smallish estate producing high-quality wines under the Réserve du Prieuré d'Antugnac and Château d'Antugnac labels.

Domaine des Astruc, Pierre et Jacques Astruc – old-established firm producing wines with more character than many. Clean, fresh, elegant wines.

Les Sieurs d'Auriac, Marc Ramires – a special *cuvée* produced by the same producer as Château d'Antugnac, mainly for restaurant use. Quite lightweight, soft, fresh wine, medium length.

Domaine Collin-Rosier – new *négociant*, founded in 1982.

Domaine de Fourn – old-established small grower, producing fuller-flavoured ripe wines.

Maison Guinot – produces attractive elegant floral wines, quite lightweight, aperitif style.

Domaine de Treilhes, Gérard Roussel – smallish estate producing well-made wines.

Cabardès, VDQS

Factfinder	
STATUS	VDQS
COLOUR	Red, rosé
SIZE OF REGION	240 hectares
AVERAGE ANNUAL PRODUCTION	10,000 hectolitres
MAXIMUM YIELD	50 hectolitres per hectare
MINIMUM ALCOHOL	11°

Grape Varieties	
CINSAULT GRENACHE MOURVÈDRE SYRAH	percentage unlimited
CARIGNAN	maximum 30 per cent
AUBUN CABERNET SAUVIGNON COT FER MERLOT NEGRETTE PICPOUL NOIR TERRET NOIR	maximum 40 per cent

This VDQS can also be labelled Côtes du Cabardès et de l'Orbiel, and covers wines from fourteen communes on the slopes of the Montagne Noir, north of Carcassonne. These wines, which are rarely seen in the UK, are often quite different in character to most other Languedoc-Roussillon wines, and may be more akin to some of the wines from south-west France. Although the principal grape varieties are those of the rest of the region, increasing use of Bordeaux varieties can produce wines that are a little more herbaceous in style. The majority of the wines are made to be drunk in their youth, and are generally at their best between two and six years old. This region gained VDQS status in 1973, but there is no obvious reason why it has not been upgraded to full AC.

The price at the cellar door is generally quite reasonable, varying from around 15-25 francs for well-made examples.

Château de Brau, Gabriel Tari – very small domaine producing soft round supple wines, with a good proportion of Merlot in the blend.

Cave Co-opérative de Conques-sur-Orbiel – one of the older co-operatives, founded in 1929. Grenache-based blend, with additions of Merlot and Syrah, producing a fuller-flavoured, quite spicy wine.

Union Co-opérative du Cabardès et du Fresque – this co-operative produces an oak-aged blend, sound, medium-bodied, from traditional local varieties, with the addition of Merlot and Cabernet.

Château de Pennautier, Comtesse de Lorgeril – old-established château, producing leaner, quite elegant wine predominantly from the Bordeaux varieties.

Château de Rayssac, Jean de Cibeins – larger domaine, producing clean, well-balanced wines that are attractive in their youth.

Château Rivals, Charlotte Capdevila-Troncin – firm, well-structured wines with a good backbone, from local varieties with the addition of Cabernet.

Clairette de Bellegarde, AOC

Factfinder	
STATUS	AOC
COLOUR	White
SIZE OF REGION	50 hectares
AVERAGE ANNUAL PRODUCTION	1,800 hectolitres
MAXIMUM YIELD	45 hectolitres per hectare
MINIMUM ALCOHOL	11.5°
Grape Varieties	
CLAIRETTE	100 per cent

Clairette de Bellegarde is a dry white wine from the commune of Bellegarde, between Nîmes and Arles. It was one of the earliest Languedoc communes to receive its appellation, in 1949, and enjoys considerable local fame.

The soil is alpine diluvium, a red, stony soil with good drainage which is said to give the wine its distinctive bouquet. Until recently the wine was mainly used for vermouth production.

This is a wine for drinking young, when it is fresh, dry, and has an attractive soft round almondy ripeness. All too often in the past the wine was rather overblown, flabby and flat, but with modern techniques, including cool fermentation, better attention to the picking date, and increasing use of temperature-controlled stainless steel tanks, the wines have become fresher and more fragrant in style. A co-operative controls a good proportion of the production, although its wines are sound rather than exciting. The vineyards had been largely abandoned in the 1960s and 1970s, but are now enjoying a renaissance, due largely to a few very good domaines producing attractive wines. Prices vary from around 15-25 francs at the cellar door.

Domaine de l'Amarine, Nicolas Godebski – fresh crisp fruity white, one of the best produced.
Cave Co-opérative 'La Clairette' – pleasant soft dry white, but often a little bland.
Domaine Saint-Louis-la-Perdrix, Philippe Lamour – another of the finest producers in this appellation; lighter and more delicate in style. Needs to be drunk young, as it loses fruit after a couple of years in bottle.

Clairette du Languedoc, AOC

Factfinder	
STATUS	AOC
COLOUR	White
SIZE OF REGION	300 hectares
AVERAGE ANNUAL PRODUCTION	12,100 hectolitres
MAXIMUM YIELD	50 hectolitres per hectare
MINIMUM ALCOHOL	11.5°

(Wines with a minimum of 14°, and aged for a minimum of three years, can be labelled *rancio*)

Grape Varieties	
CLAIRETTE	100 per cent

Clairette du Languedoc is a white wine produced in or around eleven communes on the right bank of the Hérault, whose name can be included on the label: Aspiran, Adissau, Le Bosc, Cabrières, Ceyras, Fontès, Lieuran-Cabrières, Nizas, Paulhan, Péret, and St-André-de-Sangonis. The region obtained its appellation in 1943, and was far better known in the 1940s and 1950s than it is today. The wines were even known in the UK, and P. Morton Shand mentioned in the 1950s that the wine had recently become popular in London, stating that the wine was made sweeter for the London trade than for local consumption. The area has the potential for expansion, and production is now on the increase, having diminished over the past twenty years or more.

The wine can be dry, medium dry, or even sweet, and has a quite distinctive, almost bitter bouquet. It used to be made in a maderized sherry style, and this style, called *rancio*, can still be found. The grapes are picked late in the season, when they are very ripe, verging on over-ripe. Most of the wine is dry to off-dry, full-flavoured, and is for drinking young. Because it has more powerful flavours than most whites in the region, it is popular with the strongly-flavoured local fish dishes such as *bourride sêtoise*, *brandade*, and fish stews. Average prices are between 18 and 30 francs a bottle at the cellar door.

There is also theoretically a *vin de liqueur*, made by adding 5-8 per cent of neutral alcohol at 90° during the course of fermentation. The finished wine must have at least 17° actual alcohol, with a residual sugar between 9 and 40 grains per litre. It sounds a fascinating wine, but I have been unable to track any down so far, most growers professing ignorance of its existence.

Les Vignerons d'Aspiran – the local co-operative, producing pleasant but not very distinctive wines, fresh and clean, but lacking character.
Domaine d'Aubepierre, Colette et Guy Crébassol, Nizas – quite herbaceous, rich dry white wines, attractive in their youth. Well made.
Château La Condamine Bertrand, Jany – rather fat, ripe banana fruit, off-dry, and quite distinctive whites. Unusual and well made.
Château St-André, Jean-Louis Randon – crisp light fruity young wines, well balanced.

Collioure, AOC

Factfinder	
STATUS	AOC
COLOUR	Red and rosé
SIZE OF REGION	2,200 hectares
AVERAGE ANNUAL PRODUCTION	2,300 hectolitres
MAXIMUM YIELD	45 hectolitres per hectare
MINIMUM ALCOHOL	13°
(The red wines have to be aged for a minimum of nine months before sale)	
Grape Varieties	
GRENACHE	minimum 60 per cent
MOURVÈDRE CARIGNAN	minimum 25 per cent
SYRAH CINSAULT	

Collioure is a red wine, and from 1990 a rosé also. It is the smallest AC in Roussillon. Created in 1971 in order to give the *vignerons* of the Banyuls region an AOC for their unfortified table wines, the area of the AOC is identical to that of Banyuls: the communes of Collioure, Port-Vendres, Banyuls and Cerbère, in the coastal area just to the east of the Pyrenees and the border with Spain. This region gained its reputation earlier than most Languedoc-Roussillon vineyards, as Collioure and Port-Vendres were commercial ports, and Banyuls had been shipped for a great many years. A character invented by Alexandre Dumas boasted of his purchase of a *tonneau* of wine from Collioure. In the 1960s sales of fortified wines were slow, and growers had requested an appellation for unfortified wines.

Although production is quite small, it is likely to increase dramatically now that the appellation covers rosé wines as well as red. The wines vary from light and fruity for drinking young, to full-bodied wines for ageing. Because the yields are generally small, the wines are rich, peppery and often port-like in flavour, dry but very ripe and baked. They can have the bouquet and flavour of ripe cherries, plums, and even fruit kernels. The best wines age very well, taking on slightly smoked, leathery, ripe baked fruit flavours. Well-made Collioure is one of the best reds of Languedoc-Roussillon. It is excellent with full-flavoured foods, game dishes and rich stews.

Prices vary considerably, from around 20-40 francs, and occasionally more.

Groupement Inter-co-opérative du Cru Banyuls – top-quality Collioure, sold under the label Domaine de Baillaury. The Groupement sell some 80 per cent of the appellation, as well as 95 per cent of Grand Cru Banyuls, and 50 per cent of generic Banyuls. Powerful Collioure, with rich green pepper and spice flavours which develop well with age. Well-made wines with good potential.

Cellier des Templiers – if you are not discouraged by the unusual 'hard-sell' approach here, their wine is rich and attractive, a little lighter and less baked than many.

L'Étoile – one of the better co-operatives in this region, producing solid, fruity wines which age well.

Domaine du Mas Blanc, Dr André Parcé – the most famous, and usually the most expensive, wines of the region. The wines are usually released a couple of years later than those of other producers, and require several more years ageing. Classic full-flavoured purple wines, with the flavour of ripe cherries and prunes. Made from a blend including 50 per cent Mourvèdre and 20 per cent Counoise, with some very old vines. Concentrated high-class wines.

Domaine de la Rectorie, Parcé Frères – deep opaque purple wines, with ripe peppery oaky fruit nose and palate, quite tannic when young, with a nice hint of oak maturation. Need ageing to show at their best. Several *cuvées* produced, according to the vintage.

Corbières, AOC

Factfinder	
STATUS	AOC
COLOUR	Red, rosé and white
SIZE OF REGION	14,000 hectares
AVERAGE ANNUAL PRODUCTION	720,000 hectolitres
MAXIMUM YIELD	50 hectolitres per hectare (40 hectolitres per hectare for Corbières Supérieures)
MINIMUM ALCOHOL	11.5° red and rosé, 11° white (12° for red Corbières Supérieures, 12.5° for white and rosé Corbières Supérieures)

Grape Varieties	
CARIGNAN GRENACHE TERRET NOIR MOURVÈDRE PICPOUL SYRAH CINSAULT	minimum 90 per cent for red wine
MACCABÉO BOURBOULENC GRENACHE GRIS	maximum 10 per cent
GRENACHE BLANC MALVOISIE MACCABÉO MUSCAT PICPOUL CLAIRETTE TERRET BLANC	minimum 90 per cent for red wine

Corbières produces red, white and rosé wines from the delimited mountain valley area between Lézignan, Narbonne and Roussillon, covering eighty-seven communes. The vines are planted mainly on hillsides, to give less vigorous growth. The proportions of different varieties grown vary according to the different zones within the region. Carignan has been subjected to a number of stages of reduction: if a

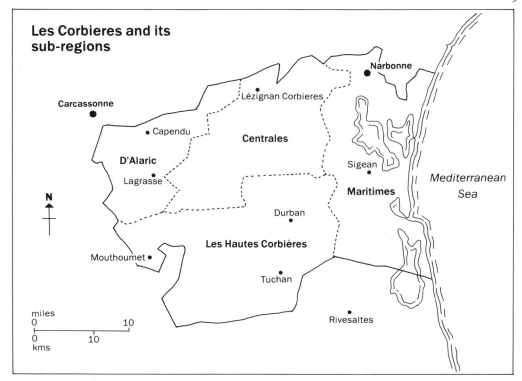

Les Corbieres and its sub-regions

vineyard has over 10 per cent Syrah and Mourvèdre, it can have up to 70 per cent Carignan; if not, it can have only up to 60 per cent. Until twenty years ago, over 95 per cent of the vineyards were planted with Carignan, but now Cinsault, Syrah, Mourvèdre and Grenache are being more widely planted.

Over 90 per cent of production is red wine, with a little rosé and only a minute proportion of white. A good proportion of the wine is sold in bulk, in bag-in-box, tetrabriks, and other containers. Sixty-two co-operatives vinify the wines of about 9,000 growers, and a further 1,000 growers vinify their own production.

The region covers over 23,000 hectares of land in the Aude *département*, from Narbonne to Carcassonne, of which approximately 14,000 hectares are planted with AC varieties. Corbières was granted VDQS status in 1951, and upgraded from VDQS to AOC in December 1985. It originally included the regions of Minervois, Fitou, La Clape and Quatourze, which now have their own appellations. The size of the region, and the enormous numbers of growers, inevitably leads to great variations in quality, and many growers would like to see the region sub-divided. Climate, soils, rainfall and topography vary tremendously, and if sub-regions were stated on the label it would give an indication of the style and quality of the individual wines. At present a few growers add the sub-region to the label, but there is little awareness of the zones, even within the region itself. Around 7.5 million cases of AC wine are produced a year.

The following are the main sub-divisions of region, as defined by the INAO.

Les Corbières Maritimes covers the coastal region, from Narbonne to Fitou, north of Rivesaltes. This region has warm winters and a cooler, semi-arid summer climate, with low rainfall. It is separated from the rest of the region by mountain ridges, and vineyards are on the lower hillsides. The wines are generally softer, lighter, and more forward in character.

Les Corbières Centrales, around the town of Lézignan-Corbières, is a drier region, producing wines with firmer structure. The vines are planted on thin, stony soils, forming a series of slopes. Increased plantations of Syrah have produced wines which age very well, and this region produces potentially some of the finest wines.

Les Corbières du Val d'Orbieu covers the hills between the *massif* of Alaric in the north and Montagne to the south. The vineyards are on quaternary terraces, around St-Pierre-des-Champs, Lézignan and Gasparets.

Montbrun, Escales covers two communes with different topography, but with a similar climate to Val d'Orbieu.

Les Corbières Montagneuses is the highest region to the south-west of the *massif*, north of Cucugnan. Vineyards are on primary shale and slate, to the highest altitude at which grapes will ripen.

Le Val de Dagne vineyards are planted on a marl depression, with Atlantic climate influences, around the communes of Villar-en-Val and Rieux-en-Val.

Les Corbières d'Alaric, in the north-west of the region, from south of Carcassonne to south of Lagrasse, is less dry than the Centrales region, with an Atlantic influence. The vineyards are on limestone-based terraces, and the wines are more aromatic in style. This area is excellent for whites and rosés.

Les Hautes Corbières, in the south-west of the region, engulfs the towns of Mouthoumet, Durban, and Tuchan. This is a very dry area, producing concentrated, full-bodied wines which age very well.

The reds are generally full-flavoured and powerful, and can age well, especially those from the Centrales and Hautes Corbières regions. An increasing proportion are, however, made by *macération carbonique*, and are lighter wines for drinking young. Although this proportion is now around 40 per cent, the method is not generally mentioned on the label. Many of the wines, however, now have a back label, with helpful information including optimum drinking age. The rosés are lighter, generally dry and fruity, and the whites can be surprisingly light and delicate in style. Prices, in line with quality, can vary from rock-bottom to expensive: 12 francs to about 50 francs, with an average of 20-30 francs at the cellar door.

The Corbières Supérieures appellation applies to a more restricted region, covering the better vineyard sites – a total of some thirty-nine communes – and it places tighter restrictions on yield. The wines can, of course, be de-classified to Corbières. Most of the estates do not bother with the Supérieures appellation, preferring to opt for a more detailed regional classification.

In a region this size, there is obviously a multitude of properties. The following are a selection of those whose wines I have tasted:

Château Aiguilloux, François and Marthe Lemarié, Thézan des Corbières – powerful, firmly structured reds for long ageing.

Ancien Comté de Durban, Caves de l'Ancien Comté de Durban – lively zesty lemony dry white, one of the nicest from the region, ripe with plenty of fruit. Also attractive but less remarkable red, with soft juicy flavours.

Château Le Bouïs, Pierre Clément, Gruissan – very well-made crisp clean whites, and excellent reds, produced from old vines. Several *cuvées* of red are produced, of which the top *réserve cuvée*, although expensive, is outstanding. Firm powerful wines for long ageing.

Château de Cabriac, Jean de Cibeins – very old property, dating from 1215. Both red and white are produced, the white being crisp, clean and fresh, pleasant but a little neutral. The red, which is produced by *macération carbonique*, and is aged in oak casks, is fruity, soft, and attractive. It can be drunk young, or aged up to five years.

Château Capendu, SCF, Granel, Arzens – lighter-style reds, approachable and forward. Well made.

Château de Caraguilhes, Lionel Faivre, St-Laurent-de-la-Cabrerisse – good-quality red, white and rosé wines, produced by organic methods.

Les Vignerons de Cucugnan, Cucugnan – good-quality red, white and rosé Corbières, as well as Vins de Pays. Generally wines for drinking young.

Château Étang des Colombes, Henri Gualco, Lézignan-Corbières – seventeenth-century estate producing well-made wines with ripe fruit flavours. Their Sélection du Bois des Dames has if anything a touch too much oak, but is nevertheless well made and of good quality. I prefer their Cuvée du Bicentenaire at half the price, if you can find it. The white also is excellent.

Château Hélène, Marie-Hélène Gau, Barbaira – run by a psychologist who turned to viticulture in 1976. An excellent range of wines, including some of the most expensive in the region.

Château de Lastours, Centre d'Aide par le Travail – this large property in Portel des Corbières is run by handicapped workers, and produces several *cuvées* – five reds as well as whites and rosé. The best reds are Cuvée Simone Descamps and Cuvée Ermengarde, which have some ageing in *barrique*. Their best white is labelled Blanc de Blancs. All their wines are consistently good to excellent.

Château de Mandourelle, Eric Latham, Villesèque des Corbières – excellent oak-aged reds, from a blend of Carignan, Cinsault, Grenache and Syrah.

Les Producteurs du Mont Tauch – this co-operative produces red and white wines. The white is from Grenache Blanc, and is fresh and well made, with clean fruit on the palate, soft, but with a little crisp acidity to balance.

Château les Ollieux – rich cedary spicy reds, soft and elegant, with good balance and length. Very well made.

Château Les Palais-Randolin, Xavier de Volontat, St-Laurent-de-la-Cabrerisse – a large estate producing powerful, well-structured reds for long ageing.

Les Producteurs Réunis de Paziols – attractive soft medium-weight red, sold somewhat confusingly under the label Domaine de Sainte-Colombe. Well-made wine for drinking in its youth.

Château de ribauté, Les Vignerons de la Montagne d'Alaric, Ribauté – produces good-quality red, white and rosé wines. The red is oak-aged.

Roque Sestrière, Jean Bérail, Ornaisons – produces one of the finest whites of the region, labelled as *vieilles vignes*.

Domaine de Trillol, Rouffiac-les-Corbières – warm plummy soft ripe reds with good balance and length.

Domaine de Villemajou, Georges Bertrand, St-André-de-Roquelongue – excellent domaine, producing full-flavoured reds with a touch of oak-ageing.

Château La Voulte-Gasparets, Patrick Reverdy, Boutenac – several *cuvées* of red, aged in oak, from the traditional blend of Carignan, Grenache, Cinsault and Syrah. Excellent-quality wines with good structure and ageing potential.

Costières du Gard/Costières de Nîmes, AOC

Factfinder	
STATUS	AOC
COLOUR	Red, white and rosé
SIZE OF REGION	3,000 hectares
AVERAGE ANNUAL PRODUCTION	200,000 hectolitres
MAXIMUM YIELD	60 hectolitres per hectare
MINIMUM ALCOHOL	11°

Grape Varieties	
MOURVÈDRE	
GRENACHE	
SYRAH	percentage unlimited for red and rosé wines
TERRET NOIR	
COUNOISE	
CARIGNAN	maximum 50 per cent
CINSAULT	maximum 50 per cent

CLAIRETTE	
GRENACHE	
UGNI BLANC	} minimum 50 per cent for white wines
MARSANNE	
ROUSSANNE	
MACCABÉO	
ROLLE	} maximum 50 per cent

This region has had its AOC since 1985. Since 1989 the vineyards to the south of the Rhône have decided to change from Costières du Gard to Costières de Nîmes – the Gard being considered part of the Rhône for promotional purposes, and Nîmes more part of the Languedoc. This can cause some confusion: while many of the estates are changing their labels to Nîmes, the placards advertising their vineyards may still be labelled Gard. Some *vignerons* are producing two *cuvées*, one under each name. The vineyards cover some 3,000 hectares of flat, stony soil between Nîmes and Montpellier.

Prices are generally very reasonable, averaging between 10 and 16 francs at the cellar door, and there are some good-quality wines. Styles vary considerably, with many red wines made by *macération carbonique*, for early drinking. 97 per cent of the production is red or rosé.

Domaine de l'Amérine, Nicolas Godebski, Bellegarde – one of the best whites of the region, made from Grenache Blanc. Also pleasant but light rosé and reds.

Château de Campuget, SA du Château de Campuget, Manduel – one of the best reds of the appellation. Fuller-flavoured than most, fruity and gentle, with good length.

Domaine des Consuls, Jean Carrières, Jonquières – firm ripe rich reds, with attractive ripe spicy flavours. Well-made wines which improve with two to five years' ageing.

Château des Fontinelles, Fayet-Manquillet, Gallician – a 63-hectare estate, producing soft, fruity, lightish reds made for drinking in their youth.

Cuvée Gagarine, Les Vignerons de St-Gilles – this co-operative produces several *cuvées*, under both the Nîmes and the Gard appellations. The Gagarine, one of their top *cuvées*, is named after the Soviet astronaut, who visited the cellar in 1967. Generally all their wines are one-dimensional.

Cave Pilote de Gallician, Vauvert – old-fashioned but good-quality co-operative producing one of the better whites of the region, and a light but attractively fruity red.

Domaine Le Grand Plaignol, Roger Marès, Manduel – spicy characterful reds with an attractive hint of oak. Among the best of the appellation.

Domaine Grand St-André, Cave des Vignerons de St-Gilles – one of the better-balanced *cuvées* from this co-operative, from a specific vineyard site. Soft, spicy and peppery, if a little short.

Domaine Ste-Colombe et les Ramaux, P. Guillon, St-Gilles – attractive elegant fruity reds for drinking within three years of the vintage.

Domaine St-Louis-la-Perdrix, GFA Mme Lamour et ses enfants – good-quality domaine in Bellegarde, producing soft, lightweight, fruity reds for drinking in their youth. Generally pleasant but a little lacking in character.

Château de la Tuilerie, Mme Serre, Bellegarde – modern vinification methods produce clean fresh rosé and whites, and light fruity reds. Well made but somewhat lightweight.

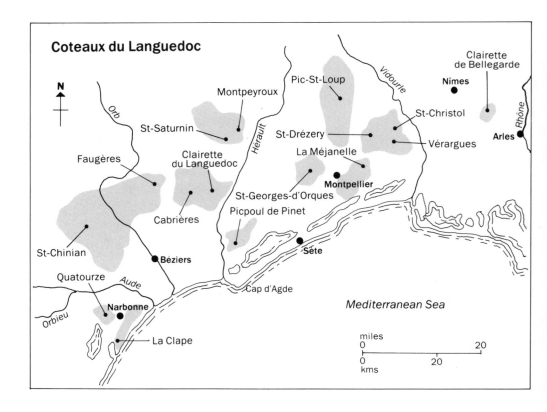

Coteaux du Languedoc, AOC

Factfinder	
STATUS	AOC
COLOUR	Red and rosé, whites in certain communes only
SIZE OF REGION	6,300 hectares
AVERAGE ANNUAL PRODUCTION	320,000 hectolitres red and rosé
	20,000 hectolitres white
MAXIMUM YIELD	50 hectolitres per hectare
MINIMUM ALCOHOL	11°

Grape Varieties	
CARIGNAN	maximum 50 per cent
MOURVÈDRE SYRAH	minimum 10 per cent
GRENACHE NOIR LLADONER PELUT	minimum 20 per cent where blend includes Carignan
CINSAULT	maximum 50 per cent
COUNOISE TERRET NOIR GRENACHE GRIS PICPOUL	maximum 10 per cent
BOURBOULENC CLAIRETTE MACCABÉO UGNI BLANC TERRET PICPOUL	as part of rosé blends only

After Corbières, this is the second largest region, covering the vineyards to the west of Nîmes, down to the coast by Montpellier, and across to Béziers. Some 120 communes produce over 4 million cases a year. The region was granted its AOC in 1985, after grouping together as a VDQS in 1963.

There is a variety of different soils and climates, and the twelve best sub-regions can hyphenate their names to the appellation. Wines without a sub-region are red or rosé, the only whites coming from the sub-regions of Pic-St-Loup, La Clape and Pinet. Many of the sub-regions have been famous for several centuries for the quality of their wines. Within this region lie also some areas that have been promoted to their own separate appellation, including Faugères and St-Chinian, and others will probably follow in time.

Quality and prices are quite varied; most wines will cost between 15 and 25 francs at the cellar door, and there are some marvellous bargains to be found in this appellation. Coteaux du Languedoc has a large number of smaller growers and estates, as well as some of the best innovative wine-making; vineyard land is relatively inexpensive here.

Domaine Simone Coudert, Neffies – soft, quite lightweight red wines, pleasant, lightly peppery, but a little undistinguished. This is a biological estate, following *Nature et Progrès* rules.

Château Coujan, Guy et Peyre, St-Chinian – quite full-flavoured dry white wine from a blend of half Rolle and half Grenache Blanc. Well made.

Château du Grès St-Paul, Lunel – attractive soft ripe reds with a good dose of Syrah. Good value.

Domaine Guiraud-Boyer, Xavier Guiraud, Causses-et-Veyran – small estate producing first-class wines. Their red, which contains a high proportion of Syrah, is firm and full-flavoured. Expensive, but very good quality.

Mas Jullien, Olivier Jullien, Jonquières (see also page 147) – one of the rising stars of Languedoc, producing red, rosé and white wines. His two red *cuvées* are Depierre, for drinking at three to five years of age, and Cailloutis, with longer ageing potential. Both are very well made, and the composition and style of both varies from vintage to vintage. His whites, one *cuvée* from Viognier and Chenin Blanc, the other from very old Carignan Blanc and Grenache Blanc vines, are in short supply, and are very well-made wines, worth seeking out.

Château Langlade, Cadene Frères, Langlade – small old-established estate producing firm full-flavoured wines for medium-term ageing.

Château St-Ferréol, Comtes Jérome et Henri d'Ormesson, Paulhan – well-made reds, elegant, with blackcurrant and mulberry fruit flavours and a hint of oak.

Prieuré de St-Jean de Bébian, Alain Roux, Pézenas – absolutely outstanding red wines for very long ageing. The only problem is that it is impossible to track down the somewhat eccentric owner in order to purchase his excellent wines. Reports from friends, both wine trade and interested amateurs, tell the same sad tale. It is hard to raise anyone in this beautiful tumbledown priory, which looks like a good set for a horror movie, and most customers go away empty-handed. The wines are made from a number of varieties, with small yields and old vines, and are reminiscent of old-style Châteauneuf-du-Pâpe; rich, broad and solid, with great class and length.

Domaine Paul Gabriel Vaillé, Salelles du Bosc – very attractive spicy smoky tarry reds, with good balance and not too much tannin.

Coteaux du Languedoc Cabrières, AOC

Factfinder	
STATUS	AOC
COLOUR	Red, rosé and white
SIZE OF REGION	250 hectares
AVERAGE ANNUAL PRODUCTION	6,500 hectolitres
MAXIMUM YIELD	50 hectolitres per hectare
MINIMUM ALCOHOL	11°

Grape Varieties	
CARIGNAN	maximum 50 per cent
CINSAULT OEILLADE	minimum 45 per cent for rosé
SYRAH MOURVÈDRE GRENACHE CLAIRETTE	maximum 5 per cent 100 per cent for white wine production

This appellation applies mainly to red and rosé wines, with a small amount of white, produced in the commune of Cabrières, to the south-east of the region of Faugères, near Aspiran, and to the north of Béziers. The vineyards are very steep, with a slate soil, and yields are generally low. Most of the wine is produced by the one co-operative.

The wines of Cabrières are warm, ripe and often quite dry and peppery in style; rustic rather than elegant, and sometimes a little lacking in finesse. However, it is a region with the potential to produce some good-quality wines. Prices vary considerably: from around 15 francs to 30 francs or more for some of the top *cuvées*.

Domaine du Temple, Maurice Muller – a small domaine making peppery warm ripe wines. Their Cuvée Jacques de Molay is superb, elegant, ripe and spicy.
Les Vignerons Réunis de Cabrières – excellent wines, especially their Cuvée Fulcrand Cabanon, named after a seventeenth-century priest who presented the wines of Cabrières to the court of Louis XIV. From a blend of Grenache, Cinsault, Syrah and Mourvèdre, it is rich, spicy, broad and plummy, with big peppery ripe fruit, and requires around five years' ageing.

Coteaux du Languedoc La Clape, AOC

Factfinder	
STATUS	AOC
COLOUR	Red, white and rosé
SIZE OF REGION	1,000 hectares
AVERAGE ANNUAL PRODUCTION	8,000 hectolitres (3,000 hectolitres white)
MAXIMUM YIELD	50 hectolitres per hectare
MINIMUM ALCOHOL	11°
Grape Varieties	
RED AND ROSÉ WINES	as for Coteaux du Languedoc
BOURBOULENC	minimum 60 per cent for white wines
CLAIRETTE	
MACCABÉO	
GRENACHE BLANC	
TERRET	

La Clape produces red, white and rosé wines, around the area of Armissan, Fleury d'Aude, Salles d'Aude, Vinassan and Narbonne. The vineyards are on a limestone outcrop, and the wines are generally medium-weight and quite perfumed. The reds are often Carignan-based; solid and tannic, needing several years' ageing. Lighter wines are those blended with Terret, Grenache and Clairette, and can be quite elegant. The whites are considered to be among the best of the region, and are surprisingly fresh and light. Prices are generally around 15-25 francs at the cellar door, with whites usually more expensive than reds.

Château de Marmorières, Vinaissan – light fresh crisp whites with a slight spritz. Clean and refreshing.

Château Moujan, Mme G. de Braquilanges – firm, quite austere gamey reds from a classical blend, including a good percentage of Carignan. Well-made wines with good ageing potential.

Château Pech-Céleyran – rich spicy red with ripe gamey fruit flavours, and just a hint of oak. Not over tannic, round, soft and rich, well made.

Domaine de Rivière-le-Haut, Jean Ségura – well-made whites, with aromatic floral fruit flavours.

Château Rouquette-sur-Mer, Jacques Boscary – excellent whites, from the Bourboulenc variety. Ripe and full-flavoured, dry but with rich fruit. Good reds, quite soft and spicy in style.

Coteaux du Languedoc Méjanelle, AOC

Factfinder	
STATUS	AOC
COLOUR	Red and rosé, little white
SIZE OF REGION	600 hectares
AVERAGE ANNUAL PRODUCTION	10,000 hectolitres
MAXIMUM YIELD	50 hectolitres per hectare
MINIMUM ALCOHOL	11°

Grape Varieties
As for Coteaux du Languedoc

This appellation can also be presented as Coteaux du Languedoc–Coteaux de la Méjanelle, and was originally part of the Costières du Gard. It covers wines produced in the communes of Mauguio, Montpellier, the Méjanelle hills, Castelnau-le-Lez and St-Aunès, and is Montpellier's local wine. The region's wines were known as Vin de Grès in the fifteenth century, and the bishops of Montpellier had vineyards in Méjanelle, as did the viticulturist Bouschet.

Although the region mainly produces red wines, there is also a small amount of rosé and white. The varieties grown are principally Carignan and Cinsault, with a little Grenache and Syrah. The soils may be quite sandy or red in colour, stony, with large smooth round boulders or *galets* in places, similar to those found at Châteauneuf-du-Pape. This whole area was originally part of the Rhône delta.

The reds are full-flavoured, deep-coloured, and rather solid. The rosés and whites can be quite perfumed, but are generally rather soft. Prices are around 15-25 francs at the cellar door.

Château de Calage, St-Aunès – ripe spicy rich reds which generally need three to five years' ageing.
Château de Flaugergues, Henri de Colbert, Montpellier – old-established property, producing well-balanced medium-weight reds, with a hint of wood ageing.
Château St-Marcel d'Esvilliers, La Treille d'Oc, Montpellier – deep ruby wines with rich spicy black cherry flavours from this young domaine.

Coteaux du Languedoc Montpeyroux, AOC

Factfinder	
STATUS	AOC
COLOUR	Red and rosé
SIZE OF REGION	350 hectares
AVERAGE ANNUAL PRODUCTION	15,500 hectolitres
MAXIMUM YIELD	50 hectolitres per hectare
MINIMUM ALCOHOL	11°
Grape Varieties	
As for Coteaux du Languedoc	

This small region covers the communes of Montpeyroux and Arboras, to the east of the St-Saturnin region. The wine was popular with the bishops of Montpellier in the fourteenth century, and Montpeyroux has a long history of high-quality wine production. Powerful, deeply coloured reds are produced mainly from Carignan, Cinsault and Grenache, grown on rocky slaty soils often in steeply sloping vineyards. Many of the vineyards have some old vines, producing small yields of top-quality wines.

There are now five producers in Montpeyroux apart from the co-operative, and several more young growers are starting to 'do their own thing'. The co-operative does not enjoy the same high reputation as many of the other co-operatives in the region, and some growers feel that they can improve the quality image of the appellation by well-made domaine-bottled wines.

Prices vary quite considerably here, with some estates charging up to 30 or 45 francs, and others only around 20 or 25.

Domaine L'Aiguelière – attractive elegant spicy wine, maybe a touch rustic, but generally quite ripe and fruity in style.
Domaine d'Aupilhac, Sylvain Fadat – a new domaine with great potential. Started on a shoestring in 1979, the 15 hectares of vines include some very old Carignan and Cinsault, as well as Grenache, and newer plantings of Syrah. They also have small plantings of Merlot, Cabernet Sauvignon, Chardonnay, Ugni Blanc, Roussanne and Marsanne. The white (from Ugni Blanc) is very aromatic, and is produced using skin maceration and cool fermentation for maximum flavour. The red is rich, spicy and full-flavoured. At present there is a slight 'identity crisis' as Sylvain Fadat experiments with cask-ageing, producing *cuvées* ranging from little or no oak to slightly over-oaked, but the overall quality is of a very high standard.
Cave Co-opérative de Montpeyroux – supple fruity reds under the Domaine du Perou label. More forward than most, simple, and less complex.

Coteaux du Languedoc, Picpoul de Pinet, AOC

Factfinder	
STATUS	AOC
COLOUR	White
SIZE OF REGION	600 hectares
AVERAGE ANNUAL PRODUCTION	13,000 hectolitres
MAXIMUM YIELD	50 hectolitres per hectare
MINIMUM ALCOHOL	11°
Grape Varieties	
PICPOUL	100 per cent

This appellation covers dry white wines from the Picpoul variety, grown in the area between Sète and Pézenas, by the Thau basin. These wines are ideal with the local seafood. At one time much of the white was from Clairette, but this has changed over the years, although a little Clairette and Terret are still grown. The region is named after the first commune to produce and market good-quality Picpoul.

Severe hailstorms around 13 May 1990 devastated about 1,000 hectares of vineyards around this area, hitting the vines just as the tender green shoots were at their most vulnerable. A workforce had to be mustered urgently to prune off all the damaged shoots back to hard, old wood, to prevent disease from spreading in the bruised vine growth. The result was a wonderful demonstration of solidarity, as men, women and children pruned the vines back to bare wood within twenty-four hours, thus probably saving the life of many of the vines. The sight of these vines in late May was very sad; after driving through a sea of vines with lush spring growth, suddenly arriving at an area of what appeared to be dead vines, without a trace of green to be seen. Luckily the vines speedily recovered, even managing to produce a small crop from their second lot of buds later in the spring.

Much of the wine is produced by the two local co-operatives, and is clean, fresh, with an attractive slightly almondy bitterness. There are around twelve growers apart from the co-operatives, and production is increasing. One or two producers have experimented with new oak, with quite encouraging results. Picpoul is generally between 16 and 25 francs a bottle, with special *cuvées* selling at around 30 francs. It is one of the best white wines of Languedoc when well made.

Les Vignerons de Ceressou – light clean dry whites with an attractive almondy bitterness on the finish. Well made but lightweight.
Domaine Claude Gaujal – light, crisp, very clean fruity white under the label Cuvée Ludovic Gaujal. Well-made wines, with good length and balance, and plenty of character. Probably one of the best of the region.

Les Vignerons Producteurs de Pinet – crisp dry whites with a slight spritz, and a floral aromatic flavour. Well made.

Domaine de Villemarin – attractive quite full-flavoured fresh appley fruit style, with more body than many.

Coteaux du Languedoc Pic-St-Loup, AOC

Factfinder	
STATUS	AOC
COLOUR	Red, white and rosé
SIZE OF REGION	750 hectares
AVERAGE ANNUAL PRODUCTION	35,300 hectolitres
MAXIMUM YIELD	50 hectolitres per hectare
MINIMUM ALCOHOL	11°
Grape Varieties	
REDS AND ROSÉS	as for Coteaux du Languedoc
CLAIRETTE MACCABÉO GRENACHE BLANC	percentage unlimited for white wines

This large vineyard region covers fourteen communes, starting some 20 kilometres to the north of Montpellier, dominated by the Pic-St-Loup mountain, which is often depicted on wine labels from this region. The area has a higher than average rainfall, around 800 millimetres, and the climate is somewhat cooler. This provides ideal conditions for varieties such as Mourvèdre and Syrah, and there are also plantations of Cabernet Sauvignon and Merlot, as well as Chardonnay and Chenin Blanc for whites. Potential here is excellent, and some of the more recent private estates show great promise.

   Large quantities of lightish red and rosé are produced from Carignan, Cinsault, Oeillade and Alicante, as well as smaller quantities of high-quality fuller-flavoured wines. Much of the wine is vinified by the five co-operatives, but the number of private domaines is growing. Whites can be attractive, with light fresh almondy young fruit flavours. Prices are generally very reasonable, at around 10-20 francs at the cellar door.

Cave Co-opérative de Claret – several reds are produced here, under different château names. Pleasant wines, generally with a high percentage of Cinsault and Carignan, and generally for drinking within three to five years.

Cave Co-opérative St-Mathieu-de-Tréviers – the largest co-operative in the region, selling the produce of the other local co-operatives as well as its own. Started in 1950, this modern co-operative sells large quantities of wine in bulk and in bag-in-the-box. Wines are generally inexpensive, everyday quality; sound but a little neutral. **Domaine de la Roque**, Jacques Boutin, Fontanes – big, full-flavoured complex reds with very good ageing potential, and a nice hint of spicy oak.

Coteaux du Languedoc Quatourze, AOC

Factfinder	
STATUS	AOC
COLOUR	Red and rosé, some white
SIZE OF REGION	250 hectares
AVERAGE ANNUAL PRODUCTION	10,000 hectolitres
MAXIMUM YIELD	50 hectolitres per hectare
MINIMUM ALCOHOL	11°
Grape Varieties	
As for Coteaux du Languedoc	

Quatourze is a small area of production on the outskirts of Narbonne, with vineyards planted on a stony quartz and sandstone outcrop, rich in iron content. It is the oldest commercial vineyard in Languedoc, and perhaps in France. Carignan is the most widely planted grape, with Grenache, Terret Noir, Cinsault, Picpoul and Blanquette as supplementary varieties. The wines are full-bodied and earthy in character, and on ageing are said to take on aromas of mushrooms and humus. These wines are still popular with *négociants*, for their deep colour and their power. A very small quantity of white is also produced from Bourboulenc. Much of the production is sold within the region, and prices are generally very reasonable, between 15 and 25 francs a bottle.

Château Notre Dame du Quatourze, M.Y. Ortola – light rosé and peppery characterful reds are produced here, from Grenache and Cinsault. Good value.

Coteaux du Languedoc Coteaux de St-Christol, AOC

Factfinder	
STATUS	AOC
COLOUR	Red
SIZE OF REGION	400 hectares
AVERAGE ANNUAL PRODUCTION	15,000 hectolitres
MAXIMUM YIELD	50 hectolitres per hectare
MINIMUM ALCOHOL	11°
Grape Varieties	
As for Coteaux du Languedoc	

This is an appellation for red wines, grown around the commune of St-Christol, to the north-east of Montpellier. This is one of the oldest vineyard regions in Languedoc, and was already famous at the time of the crusades. In 1788 the Chevalier de Suffren, the local seigneur and admiral of France, created a special barrel seal for the wines of St-Christol, to prevent fraud.

The colour of these wines is generally very purple, said to be due to some extent to the soil composition of the region, and also due no doubt to the usual combination of Carignan, Cinsault and Grenache, which form the base of most vineyards here, and include some very mature vines.

Domaine de la Coste, Luc Moynier – large modern domaine, producing several *cuvées* in most years. Their Cuvée Sélectionnée, from a majority of Syrah, is exceptional, and their normal *cuvée* also is very well made. Wines for keeping two to six years.

Domaine de Martin-Pierrat, Gabriel Martin – rich spicy full-flavoured reds, often high in alcohol.

Cave Co-opérative de St-Christol – elegant, medium-weight red with silky soft ripe fruit flavours, sold under the Cuvée Bacchus label.

Coteaux du Languedoc St-Drézery, AOC

Factfinder	
STATUS	AOC
COLOUR	Red and rosé
SIZE OF REGION	100 hectares
AVERAGE ANNUAL PRODUCTION	2,500 hectolitres
MAXIMUM YIELD	50 hectolitres per hectare
MINIMUM ALCOHOL	11°
Grape Varieties	
As for Coteaux du Languedoc	

This small region covers wines from around the commune of St-Drézery, to the north of the more famous St-Christol. Light, elegant, almost delicate fruity red wines are produced mainly from Carignan, Cinsault and Grenache, with the addition of a maximum of 15 per cent of Aramon, which is gradually being replaced by the other varieties. Most of the wine is produced by the local co-operative, and distribution is fairly localized.

Coteaux du Languedoc St-Georges-d'Orques, AOC

Factfinder	
STATUS	AOC
COLOUR	Red and rosé
SIZE OF REGION	500 hectares
AVERAGE ANNUAL PRODUCTION	12,500 hectolitres
MAXIMUM YIELD	50 hectolitres per hectare
MINIMUM ALCOHOL	11°
Grape Varieties	
As for Coteaux du Languedoc	

The region of St-Georges-d'Orques covers the north-west suburbs of Montpellier, around the communes of St-Georges-d'Orques, Murviel-lès-Montpellier, Juvignac, Lavérune and Pignan. Sadly some of the vineyards have been replaced by buildings, and parts of the area are becoming quite industrialized. One can find early nineteenth-century silver neck labels in the UK for 'St Georges', which are thought to be for wines from this region. The wines have certainly been known in the UK for several centuries; importers included the Earl of Bristol in 1715, and a number of Britons in the 1800s, who had discovered the wines while wintering in Montpellier.

The wines are mostly red, less peppery than many, with an attractive soft young fruitiness, and are principally from Cinsault, Carignan and Grenache, although there are increasing plantations of Mourvèdre, Cabernet and Merlot, most of which are vinified as Vin de Pays at present. Locals consider that the wines of St-Georges-d'Orques take on a richness and depth 'reminiscent of Chambertin' after a few years' ageing! The area has a long history of fine wine production, and was granted its own VDQS status in 1957, associating with the Coteaux du Languedoc only in 1972.

Château de l'Engarran, Mme Grill, Laverune – slightly baked peppery red wines, powerful but a little hard. Wines for medium- to long-term ageing.

Cave Co-opérative 'La Vigneronne', Pignan – medium-weight reds, with spicy ripe cherry fruit. Nicely made. Occasionally a special *cuvée* is produced, which is richer and fuller-bodied. Their Cuvée Baron d'Hebles is good.

Coteaux du Languedoc St-Saturnin, AOC

Factfinder	
STATUS	AOC
COLOUR	Red and rosé
SIZE OF REGION	500 hectares
AVERAGE ANNUAL PRODUCTION	10,000 hectolitres
MAXIMUM YIELD	50 hectolitres per hectare
MINIMUM ALCOHOL	11°
Grape Varieties	
As for Coteaux du Languedoc	

St-Saturnin is produced around the communes of St-Saturnin, Jonquières, St-Guiraud and Arboras, to the east of Lodève. It is probably one of the best known of the Coteaux du Languedoc villages, because of the hard work of the local co-operative, which was the first co-operative to sell wines directly to the consumer. Most of the wine in this region is vinified by the St-Saturnin co-operative, or the co-operative at St-Félix-de-Lodez, and there are very few growers making their own wine under this appellation.

Cave des Vignerons Réunis – lightweight wines, well made and always sound, but without great concentration. Good-value everyday 'jug' wines. They were the first to produce a *vin d'une nuit*, where the red grapes are kept on the skins for one night –

longer than for the usual rosé wine, but much shorter than for a red wine, producing a light, fruity soft red/rosé. Their other equally popular wine is the red 'Cardinal', from 50 per cent Carignan, with Grenache, Syrah, Mourvèdre and Cinsault.

Coteaux de Vérargues, or Coteaux du Languedoc – Coteaux de Vérargues, AOC

Factfinder	
STATUS	AOC
COLOUR	Red and rosé
SIZE OF REGION	1,000 hectares
AVERAGE ANNUAL PRODUCTION	5,000 hectolitres
MAXIMUM YIELD	50 hectolitres per hectare
MINIMUM ALCOHOL	11°

Grape Varieties
As for Coteaux du Languedoc

The most easterly of the Coteaux du Languedoc villages, covering nine communes around the area of Lunel and St-Séries. This is the same area which produces the Vin Doux Naturel Muscat de Lunel, and the reds are light, soft and fruity, from a base of Carignan, Grenache and Cinsault. They are generally intended for drinking in their youth. The wine was praised highly by Jean-Jacques Rousseau in correspondence to a friend. The majority of the production is vinified by the two local co-operatives, but there are also around ten other growers.

Cotes de la Malepère, VDQS

Factfinder	
STATUS	VDQS
COLOUR	Red and rosé
SIZE OF REGION	300 hectares
AVERAGE ANNUAL PRODUCTION	15,000 hectolitres
MAXIMUM YIELD	50 hectolitres per hectare
MINIMUM ALCOHOL	11°

Grape Varieties	
MERLOT	maximum 60 per cent
COT	maximum 60 per cent
CINSAULT	maximum 60 per cent
CABERNET SAUVIGNON	maximum 30 per cent
CABERNET FRANC	maximum 30 per cent
GRENACHE	maximum 30 per cent
LLADONER PELUT	maximum 30 per cent
SYRAH	maximum 30 per cent
CINSAULT	
GRENACHE	percentage unlimited
LLADONER	
MERLOT	
CABERNET SAUVIGNON	
CABERNET FRANC	maximum 30 per cent
SYRAH	

This region covers an area of thirty-one communes around Carcassonne and Limoux and is a cooler region than most of Languedoc-Roussillon, with an Atlantic influence. Nearly all the wine is produced by one co-operative.

Cave Co-opérative de Malepère – sells under several labels: Jean de Gres for their normal *cuvée* and Domaine de Foucauld for their best wine.

Côtes du Roussillon, AOC

Factfinder	
STATUS	AOC
COLOUR	Red, white and rosé
SIZE OF REGION	4,000 hectares
AVERAGE ANNUAL PRODUCTION	210,000 hectolitres red and rosé
	12,000 hectolitres white
MAXIMUM YIELD	50 hectolitres per hectare
MINIMUM ALCOHOL	11.5° red and rosé
	10.5° whites, with maximum 12°
	(maximum 3 grams per litre residual sugar for whites)

Grape Varieties

Red wines must be made from a blend of at least three grape varieties, of which the main two must not form more than 90 per cent

CARIGNAN	maximum 70 per cent
SYRAH	minimum 10 per cent
MOURVÈDRE	minimum 10 per cent
CINSAULT	
GRENACHE	
LLADONER PELUT	
MACCABÉU	maximum 10 per cent for reds
	maximum 30 per cent for rosés
MACCABÉO	
MALVOISIE	
ROUSSANNE	
MARSANNE	
ROLLE	

The Côtes du Roussillon are the most southern vineyards of France, stretching from south of Narbonne as far as the Pyrenees and covering most of the south-eastern half of the Pyrénées-Orientales *département*. This is a large appellation, covering some 117 communes and including a number of different geographical and climatic variations. The region has known several sub-divisions and re-groupings during this century, in its search for quality recognition. The Association Professionnelle des Vignerons du Haut Roussillon was formed in 1930, to delimit and defend the quality of wines in their region. In 1936 the fortified wines were granted the AC Côtes de Haut Roussillon, leading to some confusion between the names and styles of wine. The table wines, which were granted VDQS status in 1951, changed in name to Roussillon-dels-Aspres, with wines to the north of the Têt river adopting the name Corbières-du-Roussillon, and for the best sites Corbières-Supérieures-du-Roussillon. In 1972 these were re-grouped under Côtes du Roussillon, and serious efforts to upgrade and control quality led to the granting of Appellation Contrôlée status in 1977, the first of the Mediterranean VDQS to be upgraded.

The climate is Mediterranean, with hot dry summers and mild winters. Rainfall is generally low and unevenly distributed, often falling in the form of violent storms in spring and early summer. The late summer is dry, and the *tramontane* wind helps to dry the air still further, allowing the grapes to ripen very fully, and even to bake. Vines are generally *gobelet*-trained, with around 4,000 vines per hectare, and there is little mechanization. Red wines are often vinified totally or partially by *macération carbonique*, especially Carignan. At present Carignan accounts for around 70 per cent of the total plantation, although this is gradually being reduced, with plantations of Syrah and Mourvèdre increasing. Grenache is the second most widely planted variety, adding roundness and spice to the blends. Maccabéo is the principal white variety.

The region has a very long history of vine-growing: there were vineyards here at least six centuries BC. In the 1300s the kings of Spain were regular purchasers of Roussillon wines, and in the 1400s the wines were shipped to many markets through the port of Collioure. Jacques Coeur, the treasurer of France, who was based in Montpellier, made large purchases of reds and of sweet fortified wines from Roussillon. As well as producing a number of sweet fortified wines, mainly from Muscat, Grenache and Malvoisie, the region boasted a number of table wines, including apparently an aromatic dry white from the Jaumet variety, grown around Espira-de-l'Agly, whose grapes ripened at the very beginning of August.

The UK imports around 200,000 cases of Côtes du Roussillon a year, and is the third largest importer after Holland and Denmark – Holland taking a massive 43 per cent of imports.

The quantity of white wine produced in this region is increasing, although it is for the reds that the Côtes du Roussillon is famous. The red wines often have an almost port-like baked flavour which is very attractive, and can be either for drinking young, or for ageing two to three years. Whites and rosés are generally vinified at low temperatures, often in stainless steel, and are bottled within a few months to preserve their freshness. Much of the wine is produced by co-operatives, but there are also several excellent domaines.

Prices at the cellar door are very reasonable, generally between 10 and 25 francs a bottle, with some of the top domaine wines selling for 30-40 francs.

Domaine Brial, Cave des Vignerons de Baixas – one of the largest and most modern co-operatives in the region, producing some 20,000 hectolitres of Côtes du Roussillon and Côtes du Roussillon Villages. Their whites, from Maccabéo, are fresh and floral, probably the best of their range. Very good value.

Domaine Cazes Frères, Rivesaltes – excellent large private domaine, producing spicy medium-weight reds, made partially by *macération carbonique* and partly by traditional fermentation. Clean fresh whites and rosés. Good value.

Château de Corneilla, GFA Jonquières d'Oriola, Corneilla-del-Vercol – soft fruity reds which age well over three to five years. Less heavy than many.

Famille Guitard Rodor – peppery wines with good weight of fruit, and an attractive youthful ripe perfumed spicy Syrah flavour. They are grown on an unusual acid crystalline soil, in the Piémonts des Alberts.

Château de Jau, Bernard et Sabine Daure, Cazes de Pène – very large domaine producing a lighter, more elegant style of red which ages well. Less peppery in style than most, mellow and gentle, with good length. Their white, also, is gentle and perfumed in style, at its best in its youth.

Cave Co-opérative des Vins de St-André – excellent full-flavoured reds sold under the label Cuvée Louis Pasteur.

Domaine Sarda Malet, Max Malet, Les Aspres – ripe sweetish peppery jammy reds, Grenache in style. Full-flavoured, pleasant but unremarkable. Monsieur Malet has invested considerably in new cellar equipment, and his wines should be interesting to follow over the next few years.

Taïchat de Salvat, M. Salvat – attractive positive fruity reds, ripe, with a little tannin. Good length of flavour, well balanced, with some spicy smoky Syrah character on palate. Well made.

Les Maîtres Vignerons de Tautavel – Tautavel is worth visiting, not just for the museum of the prehistoric man of Tautavel, but also for several good wine producers in the village. The co-operative wines are light, cleanly made, and good value. The white is particularly good, with light, floral fruit flavours.

Cave Co-opérative de Terrats – a large percentage of their red wine (about 40 per cent) is made by *macération carbonique* of whole grapes. The wine is clean, light and fresh, agreeable, with very little tannin. Simple quaffing wine, well made, sold under the Terrassous label.

Côtes du Roussillon Villages, AOC

Factfinder	
STATUS	AOC
COLOUR	Red
SIZE OF REGION	1,400 hectares
AVERAGE ANNUAL PRODUCTION	95,000 hectolitres
MAXIMUM YIELD	45 hectolitres per hectare
MINIMUM ALCOHOL	12°

Grape Varieties	
Red wines must be made from a blend of at least three grape varieties, of which the main two must not form more than 90 per cent	
CARIGNAN	maximum 70 per cent
SYRAH	minimum 10 per cent
MOURVÈDRE	minimum 10 per cent

CINSAULT	
GRENACHE	
LLADONER PELUT	
MACCABÉO	maximum 10 per cent

This appellation covers a group of twenty-five communes with hillside vineyards, starting some 30 kilometres inland from Perpignan, along the Agly Valley, where the soils can offer more distinctive, individual wines. Part of the appellation coincides with the vineyards of the VDN Maury, and wines from these communes are often particularly spicy and peppery in style.

Two villages in this region, Latour de France and Caramany, may also hyphenate their name to the appellation, and are considered to produce exceptional wine, although this fame seems to be more historical than actual, and the majority of wines in these two communes are now produced by their respective co-operatives. One problem facing Caramany at present is that many of their vineyards may imminently be drowned by a new hydroelectric reservoir. The vineyards of Caramany are on north-facing gneiss slopes, and the wine is generally fruity, produced largely by *macération carbonique*. It is best drunk young. The vineyards of Latour de France and its neighbouring communes, on a slate soil, produce more classic Roussillon wines. Latour de France wines age well, and can be rich and peppery.

Many of the larger wine-makers in Roussillon produce both Côtes du Roussillon and Côtes du Roussillon Villages, reserving their best grapes for the Villages appellation. Thus many of the labels found need careful scrutiny, as often the difference in quality between a producer's basic wine and his Villages wine will be very noticeable. Prices are not much more for a Villages wine, with average prices from around 15-30 francs a bottle, and it is usually worth paying the extra few francs for the Villages appellation.

SCA Aglya – co-operative in the picturesque village of Estagel, producing fortified and unfortified wines. Their red is big, powerful and solid, with excellent ageing potential.
Domaine Brial, Cave des Vignerons de Baixas – Domaine Brial appears both as Côtes du Roussillon and as Villages. Although the same varieties are used for both, the Villages is traditionally vinified and spends a year in oak casks. It is a more solid structured wine which ages well. Very good value.
Cave Co-opérative de Cassagnes – well-made fat spicy rich dry reds with plenty of character. Their Cuvée des Capitelles is particularly good.
Domaine Cazes – medium-weight reds, with quite long ageing, partially in new oak vats. Elegant and quite forward in style, from a blend of Grenache, Carignan, Syrah and Mourvèdre.
Domaine des Chênes, Alain Razungles, Vingrau – peppery spicy very dry style of red, a little too dry for my taste.

Cave Co-opérative de Lesquerde – fat earthy spicy reds. Their special Cuvée Georges Pous is well made, with a pronounced gamey flavour.

Les Vignerons de Maury – light fruity reds, a little baked and plummy, pleasant but rather clumsy in style.

R. Mounié et Ses Filles, Tautavel – attractive, quite lightweight wines under the Cuvée de l'Homme de Tautavel label. Good value.

Cave Co-opérative de Tautavel – soft spicy dry reds, medium length and quality.

Faugères, AOC

Factfinder	
STATUS	AOC
COLOUR	Red and rosé
SIZE OF REGION	1,400 hectares
AVERAGE ANNUAL PRODUCTION	60,000 hectolitres
MAXIMUM YIELD	50 hectolitres per hectare
MINIMUM ALCOHOL	11.5°
Grape Varieties	
CARIGNAN	maximum 40 per cent
SYRAH MOURVÈDRE	minimum 20 per cent
GRENACHE LLADONER PELUT	minimum 20 per cent
CINSAULT	maximum 60 per cent

The Faugères appellation covers seven villages, and a surprisingly small number of growers. Only around twenty producers market their own wines, the rest selling to three co-operatives, of which Laurens is the most important. Faugères was granted its appellation in 1982, one of the earlier Coteaux du Languedoc appellations. Because of the small number of producers, the quality is more consistent, and is more easily monitored than in a larger region. Faugères has a deservedly high reputation in the region, and it is hard to go wrong when choosing a wine with this appellation.

Earlier this century, Faugères was better known for its brandy than for its wine, and since the wines for distilling were white rather than red, the region was planted with Terret, Carignan Blanc and Clairette. It also produced quantities of fortified Muscat. In the 1940s and 50s the main red vines planted were Carignan, with a little Grenache and Alicante. The area under vines was much smaller than today, and sheep and goats were more in evidence than vineyards. Gilbert Alquier was one of the first to experiment with other varieties, planting Syrah in the 1960s, as well as Mourvèdre, 'just to see how they worked'. Today, these two varieties are among the recommended varieties for the region.

At the beginning of the 1970s severe storms destroyed a number of old terraced vineyards, and SAFER, the Société d'Aménagement Foncier et d'Établissement Rural, the body responsible for viticulture and agriculture, contributed funds enabling some 80 hectares of good *garrigue* land to be cleared and planted, mainly with Grenache, and a little Syrah and Cinsault.

With the thin, slaty shale soil, relatively high altitude of around 250 metres, and south-facing slopes, the old Carignan vines produced excellent-quality wines, although the variety became more and more despised as fashions in viticulture changed.

There are two basic styles of Faugères; young, supple fruity reds produced by *macération carbonique*, and the more traditionally vinified, firm, tannic, austere wines with excellent keeping abilities, which start to show at their best four to five years after the vintage and will age well for many more years. Faugères is one of the more expensive appellations, with some of the top *cuvées* selling for between 30 and 45 francs at the cellar door, but the quality level makes these prices extremely reasonable.

Quantities for both red and rosé are increasing annually, and Faugères is quite rightly a very fashionable region. Many of the producers are making outstanding wines. About a third of the production is sold to private clients, a very high percentage for this part of the world.

For those visiting Faugères, there is a cheerful restaurant named the Bel Air which offers a menu at 55 francs including wine (1990 price). The service is slow, and we could have sworn that our *coq au vin* was based on lamb, but the food is plentiful and good, and the carafe wine is excellent. For a better choice of wine, the restaurant at Château de Grézan has a well-chosen range of Faugères, and not a single Bordeaux or Burgundy on the list.

Château des Adouzes, G.I.E. Benezech & Fils, Jean-Claude Estève – oak-aged red, with rich ripe fruit, and the mouthwatering ripeness of well-vinified Grenache and Carignan grapes. Well made.
Gilbert Alquier – good-quality red and rosé wines, with a high percentage of Mourvèdre in the blend, and yields limited to around 30 hectolitres per hectare. Clean and well-made rosés, and concentrated reds with just a hint of oak, spicy, smooth and smoky, with good ageing potential. Generally reds are at their best between three and six years of age.
Château des Estanilles, Michel Louison, Lenthéric-Cabrerolles – one of the best producers in this excellent appellation. Carefully vinified wines with rich concentration of flavour. Reds are from a blend of Syrah and Mourvèdre, with a little

Cinsault and Carignan, and take at least five to eight years to reach their peak. Whites from Maccabéo and Grenache Blanc, vinified with some skin contact, are soft and fruity, with excellent flavour. There is also a small production of an excellent and unusual rosé, produced from Grenache and aged in new oak. (Only about 500 bottles!) This property's wines are not easy to find, as most of the *cuvées* are limited, and sales are generally to private customers and to a few favoured restaurants. Monsieur Louison is starting to gain a reputation, having won a number of medals and awards, and generally there is a long waiting list for his wines.

Château La Gineste, Jean Rigaud – traditionally vinified reds, somewhat more delicate and less weighty than many.

Château de Grézan – soft attractive fruity reds under their usual *cuvée*, and a more exciting, ripe peppery wine with a hint of oak under the label Cuvée Arnaud Lubac. Château de Grézan is one of the largest producers, with a range of wines including Vins de Pays from Merlot, Pinot Noir and Chardonnay. Grézan is one of the best-set-up vineyards for visitors, and also has a restaurant, offering some of the best wines of the region.

Château Haut Fabrègues – ripe peppery full-flavoured dry reds with firm structure, which require five to eight years' ageing. Well made. Also attractive fruity rosés.

Les Producteurs Réunis de Laurens – top-quality co-operative producing several labels, including Château de Laurens and Cuvée Valentin Duc. The Château de Laurens is firm and full-flavoured, with a good proportion of Syrah, and the Valentin Duc is a little softer and rounder. Both are excellent. A future problem with Château de Laurens is that the owner of some 20 hectares of the château vineyard has decided to desert the co-operative and make his own wine, which he also wishes to call Château de Laurens. We may well see two *cuvées* with that name on the market in the future.

Château la Liquières – very attractive rich spicy gamey reds, with a touch of new oak and the smoky flavours of young Syrah.

Domaine Raymond Roque – old-established family vineyards producing traditionally made solid, firm reds with a little oak-ageing.

Fitou, AOC

Factfinder	
STATUS	AOC
COLOUR	Red
SIZE OF REGION	2,000 hectares
AVERAGE ANNUAL PRODUCTION	60,000 hectolitres
MAXIMUM YIELD	40 hectolitres per hectare
MINIMUM ALCOHOL	12°

Grape Varieties	
CARIGNAN GRENACHE	minimum 90 per cent (but with a maximum of 75 per cent Carignan)
CINSAULT MOURVÈDRE SYRAH TERRET NOIR MACCABÉO	maximum 10 per cent

Fitou was the first red table wine of the region to receive its Appellation Contrôlée, in 1948. To the south-east of the Corbières region, there are two quite distinct vineyard regions of Fitou: one by the coast between Narbonne and Perpignan, covering five communes including Fitou itself and Leucate; the other further inland, covering four communes around Tuchan and Paziols. The soils are based on limestone and slate, and the hot summer climate is mitigated by sea breezes and humidity.

These vineyards are among the best in the region, and were originally grouped under the name Fitou because this was the commune whose wines usually fetched the highest bids early this century. At that time it was thought that the name would not catch on in the UK, as it was considered 'too skittish', and the wine was usually sold as Hautes Corbières, with Fitou added in smaller lettering. However, the experts have proved quite wrong in their assessment, and Fitou is a name that has now become quite trendy in the UK.

There are only eight cellars grouped within the appellation, and around 90 per cent of the production is vinified by the seven co-operatives. Most of the wine is bottled in the unattractive traditional Fitou bottles, rather similar to some of the Provence skittle bottles, and, not content with that, most of the labels are old-fashioned and badly designed.

The wines have to be wood-aged for a minimum of nine months; a classic Fitou is gamey and spicy, with an animal nose when mature, and with good tannin and structure. Theoretically it is one of the longest-ageing reds of the Languedoc. Traditionally made wines are often rather austere in their youth, but develop well with five to eight years bottle age. Many of the wines are produced in a rather anonymous lighter style, ready to be drunk sooner. Wines are generally between 20 and 35 francs a bottle at the cellar door, which is good value for the traditionally made wines and poor value for the lighter wines.

Les Maîtres Vignerons de Cascatel – spicy, gamey, powerfully structured reds from this very good co-operative. Wines with excellent ageing potential.
Paul Colomer, Tuchan – big, powerful reds with gamey smoky flavours and

excellent ageing potential. At their best after five to seven years' ageing.

Herpé Père et Fils, *négociant* – broad, earthy red under the Cuvée Prestige label. Quite gamey and spicy, with plenty of character. Needs five to ten years to show at its best.

Les Producteurs du Mont Tauch – one of the oldest co-operatives in the region, founded in 1913. The Mont Tauch co-operative vinifies around a quarter of the production of Fitou. Pleasant, soft, forward style of wine. Since 1987 this co-operative has also vinified the wines of Château de Ségure, which are aged in oak, and are rich and concentrated.

Château de Nouvelles, Tuchan – one of the larger domaines in Fitou. These wines are ripe and spicy, medium-weight, and quite baked in style.

Cave de Paziols – medium-weight reds which benefit from two to three years ageing.

Cave Pilote des Producteurs de Villeneuve les Corbières – big, solid gamey reds with excellent ageing potential.

Limoux, AOC, dry white

Factfinder	
STATUS	AOC
COLOUR	White
SIZE OF REGION	1,360 hectares
AVERAGE ANNUAL PRODUCTION	60 hectolitres
MAXIMUM YIELD	7,500 kilos of grapes per hectare
MINIMUM ALCOHOL	10°
Grape Varieties	
MAUZAC	percentage unlimited
CHARDONNAY CHENIN BLANC	maximum 20 per cent

The appellation Limoux covers still dry white wines from the same area as the sparkling Blanquette de Limoux. As with Blanquette, the yield is limited to 7,500 kilograms of grapes per hectare, and a maximum of 100 litres per 150 kilograms is allowed. Production is very limited so the wine is not often found outside the area. It is sometimes sold as Vin de Pays de l'Aude.

Minervois, AOC

Factfinder	
STATUS	AOC
COLOUR	Red, rosé and white
SIZE OF REGION	18,000 hectares
AVERAGE ANNUAL PRODUCTION	265,000 hectolitres
MAXIMUM YIELD	50 hectolitres per hectare
MINIMUM ALCOHOL	11°

Grape Varieties	
SYRAH MOURVÈDRE GRENACHE NOIR LLADONER PELUT	minimum 30 per cent with Syrah and Mourvèdre forming a minimum 10 per cent for red and rosé wines
GRENACHE CINSAULT PICPOUL NOIR TERRET NOIR ASPIRAN NOIR CARIGNAN	maximum 60 per cent
BOURBOULENC MACCABÉO	minimum 50 per cent for white wines
PICPOUL CLAIRETTE GRENACHE BLANC TERRET BLANC LISTAN BLANC MUSCAT	

One of France's oldest vineyards, Minervois was granted appellation status only in February 1985, after struggling as a VDQS since 1951. It is a region of sixty-one communes in the *départements* of Aude and Hérault, where vineyards were probably first planted by the Benedictines and were developed during the eighth century by the bishop Benoît d'Aniane, who granted concessions to develop vineyards associated with abbeys throughout the region. The land was rented to peasants, who were assured a sale of their wine to the abbeys. These vineyards prospered until the siege of the Cathars by Simon de Montfort in the thirteenth century. Minervois abounds with

Romanesque chapels, and with interesting old churches dating from the time of Catharism. Outside the picturesque small town of Minerve, after which the region is named, stand the remnants of an enormous sling used to break down the walls when the town was under siege.

Most of the production is of red wines, with small but growing proportions of rosé and white. Minervois was planted with a large percentage of Carignan, especially during the 1950s, but more attempts are now being made to match different grapes to different soils. There was also a small but elusive production of Vin Noble de Minervois until earlier this century, but this seems to have vanished completely. This wine, highly praised by P. Morton Shand, was a high-strength red or white, with at least 13°, from Muscat, Maccabéo, Malvoisie or Grenache.

Geographical and climatic differences are quite marked through the region, which is divided into zones by way of geology, climate and rainfall. Even within individual zones, there are differences in climate, altitude and soil texture, structure and depth, and the zones have been further sub-divided. Throughout the region, the *Cers* wind from the north-west and the sea wind from the east moderate the climate to a greater or lesser degree.

East Minervois, around the town of Ginestas, is a cooler region tempered by sea winds and by rain. Occasional and often brutal storms can be a hazard in the spring and early summer. The soil is pebbly and stony, and the wines are generally fruity and aromatic.

Central Minervois is the largest region, covering most of the southern half of the appellation. The climate is hot and dry, similar to parts of southern Spain. The wines are richer and stronger in flavour.

North Minervois is the middle of the northern part of the appellation, between Caunes Minervois and Azillanet. This is a very hot area, vines being exposed southwards on the slopes, and the wines are very peppery and full-flavoured.

Haut Minervois is the region around the town of Minerve, where the vineyards are at a higher altitude and benefit from a cooler mountain climate. The wines are rich and full-flavoured, with good balance.

West Minervois is a small region where the climate is generally warm and humid, influenced by ocean breezes, and with higher rainfall. The wines are more forward.

Within these regions are a number of geographical sub-divisions, and attempts have been made to match each *terroir* with the most suitable grape varieties. While it may not be wise to subdivide the region too ruthlessly, there is no doubt that there are strongly marked regional differences in the wines produced.

The *Serres* region covers a stony plateau, with a light, limestone-based slope. The region is hot and semi-arid, with a mild spring and low rainfall, but generally a long growing season. Wines are mostly Carignan-based, with Grenache and Mourvèdre. Whites are from Bourboulenc and Maccabéo.

L'Argent Double lies to the west of Serres, in the heart of the Minervois. It can be the driest region of the Minervois, and often lacks water by September. There are various soil types, including *Les Mourels* to the east, with characteristic reliefs, rock ridges and depressions. To the south-west of l'Argent Double and its tributaries, around Caunes and Rieux Minervois, are some good but often shallow vineyard soils, with limited water reserves.

Les Piémonts du Causse or Petit Causse has south-facing slopes of marl and friable limestone, sheltered from the Cers. Good wines can be produced here when the vine varieties can withstand the drought and the heat. Carignan and Grenache are grown on the marl soils, and Cinsault on sandstone. Some Mourvèdre is planted on warm soils, which promote earlier ripening, and some Syrah on colder soils.

La Clamoux, in the west of the Minervois, has a more temperate winter, with a Mediterranean influence and moderate rainfall. This is a cooler region, at a higher altitude, and the wines are made from a Grenache base with some Syrah. Carignan is less fine here, except on well-exposed drier soils. Whites are from Marsanne and Roussanne.

Le Causse, in the north-east of Minervois, has a Mediterranean climate, but with a cold spring, and cold air from the Montagne Noire. Vines are grown on the more sheltered sites, for example around St-Jean-de-Minervois, and the slow warming in the spring leads to a shorter ripening period. The soils are very stony, with pockets of red clay limestone. Reds are Grenache- and Carignan-based, with some Syrah. Whites are from Maccabéo, Marsanne and Roussanne.

Les Côtes Noires, in the north-west of the Minervois, is a higher-altitude region where the Atlantic influence tempers the Mediterranean heat, as in Cabardès, and where rainfall is higher. The ripening cycle is shorter, and wines are generally based on Grenache and Syrah, with Carignan grown only on the slopes with the best exposure and drainage. This area is particularly successful for whites, from Marsanne, Roussanne, Chasan, Listan and Sauvignon.

All these divisions and sub-divisions can be very confusing for the consumer, and the growers' interests may be better served by promoting the region as a whole. In 1977 a syndicate of producers was formed to help promote the name of Minervois.

It is hard to generalize on style for such a large appellation, but the wines tend to be a little lighter and gentler in style than Corbières. Quality varies considerably, as do prices. Wines can be found from as little as 8-10 francs, up to around 25 francs a bottle at the cellar door.

Château Bassanel, P. Jeanjean, Olonzac – attractive ripe full-flavoured reds which age well.

Château Coupe-Roses, Jacqueline & Françoise Le Calvez, Caunette – a very pretty label, and a rather lightweight, pleasant but undistinguished red wine.

Daniel Domergue – Daniel Domergue rented vineyard land in Trausse-Minervois until 1990, and produced some excellent wines. When his lease expired, he found a

15-hectare domaine in the Haut Minervois. His wines may be found in many of the top restaurants in the region, and are big, broad and peppery, rather unyielding in their youth, but with plenty of power and flavour.

Château de Gourgazaud, La Livinière – well-made red wines with a good proportion of Syrah. Rustic and full-bodied. At their best with five to eight years' ageing.

Les Vignerons de Haut Minervois, Azillanet – rather hard, stalky reds under the label *vieilli en fût*. The oak is present, but the wines lack fruit.

Domaine Meyzonnier, Cuvée des Pierres Blanches, Jacques Pouzols, Minervois – well-made spicy peppery reds with rich Syrah and Grenache flavours.

Domaine Ste-Eulalie – red, white and rosé of good regular quality. The white is oak-aged, and is regarded as one of the best of its appellation, although I found the oak a little too marked for my taste. The rosé is excellent; fresh, dry, grapey and very thirst-quenching. The red is quite soft and forward, but with plenty of flavour, and a soft round fruitiness that is very appealing.

Domaine de Michel Sigé, Michel Sigé, St-Jean-de-Minervois – lighter-weight reds for early drinking.

Domaine Tailhades Mayranne, André Tailhades, Minerve – big, broad, rich reds which age well over five to eight years.

Château Villerambert-Julien, Marcel Julien, Caunes-Minervois – elegant firm dry reds with good length and structure. Very reliable property producing classic wines.

St-Chinian, AOC

Factfinder	
STATUS	AOC
COLOUR	Red and rosé
SIZE OF REGION	2,000 hectares
AVERAGE ANNUAL PRODUCTION	55,000 hectolitres
MAXIMUM YIELD	50 hectolitres per hectare
MINIMUM ALCOHOL	11.5°

Grape Varieties	
CARIGNAN	maximum 50 per cent
SYRAH MOURVÈDRE LLADONER PELUT GRENACHE	minimum overall 35 per cent, with a minimum 20 per cent of Lladoner and Grenache, and a minimum 10 per cent of Syrah and Mourvèdre
CINSAULT	

The St-Chinian region covers twenty communes within the Coteaux du Languedoc. Its wines have a long and proud history, and have been praised in documents as far back as 1300. After being granted VDQS status in 1945, St-Chinian was granted its own appellation in 1982. The region lies to the north of Béziers, at an altitude of between 120 and 200 metres, with a series of gently sloping south-facing vineyards on slate-based soils to the north and stonier limestone and clay-based soils further south.

Carignan, Grenache and Cinsault are the most widely planted varieties, with increasing plantations of Syrah and Mourvèdre over the last ten or twenty years. The wines are similar in style to those of Faugères, just to the north, but generally without the same depth. Some of the best estate wines are of excellent quality, and St-Chinian contains one of the best co-operatives in the whole of France: Cave Coteaux du Rieu-Berlou, where innovation is combined with tradition to produce a superb range of wines.

Prices vary considerably, from around 18-30 francs or more for the top *cuvées*.

Clos Bagatelle, M. et Mme Simon – good small domaine with a little museum, producing soft spicy wines with an attractive hint of oak-ageing.
Château Cazals-Vieil – ripe smoky spicy reds, quite soft and forward in style, but well made. Reds contain around 45 per cent Syrah. At their best between three and eight years old.
Château Coujan, Guy et Peyre – very traditional domaine, producing strong, spicy, gamey wines which age superbly. Strong believers in Mourvèdre, their wines have the typical gamey peppery ripeness of this grape. The best *cuvée* in each vintage is the Cuvée Marquise Gabrielle de Spinola, named after the former seigneur of the village, who traditionally had the first 500 litres of Coujan's best wine each year as part of the rent.
Domaine Madalle, St-Nazaire-de-Ladarez – ripe mellow fruity wines with just a touch of wood. Medium-weight.
Château Moulinier – youthful fruity-style reds, attractive drinking when young. Less complex in style.
Cave Coteaux du Rieu-Berlou – very modern co-operative producing a range of

top-quality wines at very reasonable prices. Their Schisteil is particularly good, as is their Berloup. The vineyards are on decomposed shale soils, giving distinctive wines. **Cave Co-opérative de Roquebrun** – another co-operative that produces high-quality wines and repeatedly wins top awards in wine shows. Their vineyards are also on decomposed shale soils, and they produce ripe peppery spicy wines. The Cuvée Charlemagne is particularly fine.

Vins Doux Naturels

Vins Doux Naturels are a range of fortified wines, always high in alcohol, with a minimum of 15° and sometimes with 17° or 18°. In France they are often served as aperitifs, but they are also excellent with cheeses and desserts, and some can accompany meats and even fish dishes.

Vins Doux Naturels in their current form owe their origin to Arnaldo da Villanova, a thirteenth-century sage and doctor from Montpellier, who introduced the still from Moorish Spain and was the first to add spirit to wine to keep the natural sugar in the finished wine. His *De Vinis*, one of the first wine-making treatises, mentions the use of alcohol to stop fermentation and to prevent the wine from becoming troubled. At that time this technique was used in Roussillon and in Catalonia.

In the normal course of events the sugar in grape juice is converted into alcohol by the action of yeasts, and since most ripe grapes contain only sufficient sugar to form between 10° and 15° alcohol, most wines are naturally dry when the yeasts have completed their work. However, at around 15° the yeasts are killed off by the alcohol they have produced, and if the wine still contains some sugar at that stage, it will be sweet. If spirit is added to the grape juice during the course of fermentation, then less sugar will be converted by the yeasts before the 15° limit has been reached, and the finished wine will be sweeter. The sweetness will be that of natural grape sugar, hence Vin Doux Naturel.

Originally many of these styles of wine were produced from grapes so high in natural sugar that they had no need of further additions of spirit. The high sugar level was achieved either by picking very late in the autumn, by partially drying the grapes after picking, or by twisting the stems of the grape bunches on the vine to dry the grapes partially into raisins, thus concentrating the sugar by evaporating some of the water content. This process was known as *passerillage*, and although labour-intensive was quite widely practised in the Languedoc-Roussillon region. The grape must used in those days is recorded as attaining over 300 grams per litre of natural sugar.

The Greeks and the Romans were probably responsible for the start of this fashion in wine production. Roman recipes mention *passerillage*, and also the use of both grape concentrate and honey to make a sweet style of wine. Vinum Apianum Rivesaltimum was a popular wine of the region in Roman times. Sweet strong wines, which have

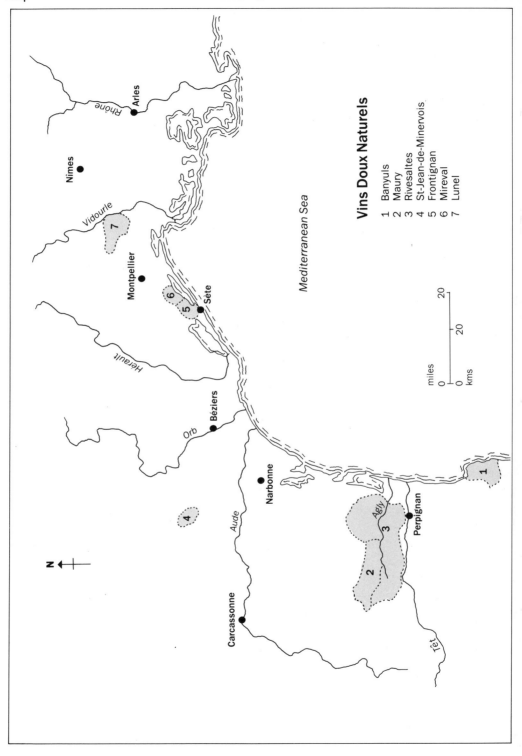

Vins Doux Naturels

1 Banyuls
2 Maury
3 Rivesaltes
4 St-Jean-de-Minervois
5 Frontignan
6 Mireval
7 Lunel

been traditional in the warmer Mediterranean regions for many centuries, can be produced only in the hottest, most southerly regions of France. Greece, Cyprus and Spain were the best producers in the sixteenth and seventeenth centuries, after which France's reputation started to grow, with Frontignan and Rivesaltes becoming the most highly regarded wines.

Apart from Muscat de Beaumes de Venise and Rasteau, both from the Rhône Valley, French Vins Doux Naturels are made exclusively in the Languedoc-Roussillon region, where the climate is sufficiently warm to ripen the grapes. The average annual temperatures are 13.5° for Maury, 16° for Banyuls and 14.5° for the rest of Roussillon, with long, hot dry summers.

It is only since the introduction of legislation early this century that the old methods of production have been forbidden, and to quality for the Vin Doux Naturel designation, the wine must be fortified with alcohol. A Vin Doux Naturel can no longer be a *vin 'naturellement' doux*. A few producers still vinify small quantities of naturally sweet wine, but this falls outside any of the Appellation Contrôlée categories and can therefore only be sold as an anonymous alcoholic beverage; it is not Vin Doux Naturel, because it has no added spirit, it is not table wine because its strength is over 15° – it is therefore taxed on the amount of alcohol it has produced, in the same way as a vermouth or aperitif wine is taxed.

Fortification has to be with neutral spirit, at a minimum of 96°, which is carried out under government supervision. The spirit is supplied by the state, and is a state monopoly. The grower has to register his intent to fortify, and arrange for a supervisor from the Régie des Alcools to be present. The wine must form not less than 5 per cent natural alcohol before fortification is carried out, and not more than 10 per cent. As the fermentation period is relatively short, this presents the grower with somewhat of a problem; the inspector must visit him on the precise day, preferably the precise hour, when he is ready to add spirit to his wine. This problem is often overcome by forming a separate vat of *mistelle*, unfermented grape juice, which is fortified with the total spirit needed for the entire stocks. This is known as a *dénaturation*, and the quantity fortified must represent at least 50 per cent of the total must. This fortification takes place under supervision, and the grower is then at liberty to add the vat to the rest of his wine at the precise moment that suits him, without further supervision. The added spirit must form a minimum of 5 per cent of the finished product, and a maximum of 10 per cent. It can be added in stages, or all at once, and the amount and precise stage of addition will determine the finished wine's sweetness. The wine-maker uses tables which give him the percentage of alcohol to add, and the must density, depending on the style of wine required.

Formerly fermentation was stopped with sulphur dioxide at the desired point, until the cellarmaster was ready to add the alcohol, but luckily this is not done nowadays.

Growers pay taxes only on the alcohol content of the spirit used, not on the alcohol of the finished wine. However, if the wine surpasses 18° in actual alcohol, then the taxes charged are doubled. When the Loi Pams, the origin of Vins Doux Naturels legislation, was passed in April 1898, growers did not pay the full tax on the alcohol used as long as the finished wine did not exceed 15°, after which they were penalized to the extent of double the tax. This was the law that first limited Vins Doux Naturels to those which had added alcohol, and excluded unfortified wines. In 1921 the law was amended to allow Vins Doux Naturels to attain between 15° and 18° inclusive, and in 1935 Vins Doux Naturels were among the first wines to receive their Appellation Contrôlée.

The grape varieties used for the production of Vins Doux Naturels are few in number. They must be capable of ripening sufficiently to attain a certain minimum sweetness in the finished wine, and must be of sufficient quality to provide a wine with personality and character. The varieties permitted are Grenache, Muscat, Maccabéo and Malvoisie. For some appellations a small percentage of other varieties is allowed in the blend.

White grapes are generally de-stemmed before pressing. Muscat grape must is sometimes left to macerate with the skins for a few hours to extract more intense aromas, otherwise white grapes are fermented apart from the skins. The temperature is carefully monitored, and should not exceed 20°C. The spirit is added once the wine has reached at least 5° natural alcohol, depending on the sweetness required. Muscat wines are allowed to be marketed from the January after the vintage, because the style should be young and fresh. Other whites are sometimes allowed a little ageing, although Maccabéo is often sold young and fresh as well. The young fresh styles will generally be vinified in stainless steel or other inert tanks, while other whites may be aged in wood to allow a little oxidation. Apart from Muscat, most white varieties need a minimum one year's ageing.

Young Muscat Vin Doux Naturel is generally grapey, floral, aromatic and charming. It needs to be drunk within a couple of years, after which it starts to become tired and to lose its flavour. In the last century Muscat was sometimes aged in wood, adding other flavours of toffee, honey and caramel to the grape flavours, more in the style of Sétubal or Australian liqueur Muscat. A few producers still age their Muscat, although they forfeit the right to the AC by doing so. In theory, they could produce a more interesting and complex wine than the AC wine, although I have not found a very exciting aged Muscat to date. I have, however, tasted Muscat Vins Doux Naturels from the last century which were far superior to anything produced from this grape today.

Red varieties are usually de-stemmed also, to prevent the harsh flavours that the stems can give, especially with added alcohol. Fermentation starts as for a normal red wine. For the less expensive younger types of red Vin Doux Naturel, the wine is pressed and the spirit added to the juice after pressing. For the better wines, and those intended for long ageing, alcohol will be added while the skins are still present. This is known as *mutage sur marc*, or *macération sous alcool*, and helps to extract more aroma, colour and tannin. The skins are generally left about ten to fifteen days in contact with the fortified wine. This method is more costly and more difficult to control, and some of the alcohol will be retained by the solids after pressing and therefore wasted. It does, however, give a better result. Reds then receive a minimum of one year's ageing, with longer for some appellations.

The different styles are labelled *doux* if the finished wine has over 90 grams per litre residual sugar, *demi-doux* with between 70 and 90 grams, and *sec* with between 35 and 70 grams. The wines may also be labelled *rancio* where they have been aged, usually in wood, but sometimes in large glass carboys known as *bonbonnes*. Ageing is sometimes done on a system similar to the Spanish *solera*, refilling barrels with the new wine as the older wine is drawn off.

Vins Doux Naturels account for 23 per cent of the agricultural revenue of the Pyrénées-Orientales, and two-thirds of the viticultural production (Banyuls 5 per cent, Maury 7 per cent, Muscat 15 per cent and Rivesaltes 73 per cent). The majority (95 per cent) of French Vins Doux Naturels come from Roussillon, and Vins Doux Naturels account for some 65 per cent of Roussillon's AC production, although only 2 per cent of that of Languedoc. The French drink three times more Vins Doux Naturels than port, whisky, and wine-based aperitifs put together, but much of this is of the lower price and quality range.

Apart from Vins Doux Naturels, other sweet wines with similar alcohol can be found in Languedoc-Roussillon, but these do not benefit from Appellation Contrôlée.

Vin Cuit

Vin cuit is a wine made from grape juice that has been heated to evaporate water and so concentrate sugars. The juice is then fermented, and alcohol may be added to stop the fermentation and leave more sweetness if required. This was a traditional home-made drink that growers produced on a very small scale for family consumption. It was drunk on festive occasions, such as Christmas Eve. A few producers make this wine commercially, although usually on a very small scale.

Carthagène

Carthagène is a traditional wine which has been produced in Languedoc for many years. It is made in the same way as Pineau de Charentes, by adding alcohol to unfermented grape juice and then usually ageing the resultant blend in wood. Either red or white grapes may be used, and the alcohol can be added to either the crushed grapes or to the juice. A number of producers have a Carthagène on their list, and these wines can be very attractive. Some producers even have more than one style, depending on the amount of wood ageing. Carthagène is generally served as an aperitif.

Vin Doux de Liqueur

This is a poor man's Vin Doux Naturel, produced from grapes that did not quite make the grade, and were either not sweet enough or have been vinified by means of adding alcohol right at the beginning, before the fermentation has started. Muscat is the usual variety used, as its grapiness suits this style of wine. *Vin doux de liqueur* may be allowed within the appellation, in which case the minimum richness, which is lower than for Vin Doux Naturel, will be stipulated. Wines without the appellation may simply be sold as 'Muscat', with a brand name. They are generally less expensive, and the flavour may not be all that different from a Vin Doux Naturel. Some may be wood-aged, and are then quite different, with a slightly caramel, almost sherry-like flavour.

Banyuls, AOC, Vin Doux Naturel

Factfinder	
STATUS	AOC, VDN
COLOUR	Red, tawny and a little white
SIZE OF REGION	2,250 hectares
AVERAGE ANNUAL PRODUCTION	36,500 hectolitres
	7,000 hectolitres Banyuls Grand Cru
MAXIMUM YIELD	30 hectolitres per hectare
MINIMUM ACTUAL ALCOHOL	15°
MAXIMUM ACTUAL ALCOHOL	18°
MINIMUM POTENTIAL ALCOHOL	21.5°
MINIMUM SUGAR AT HARVEST	252 grams per litre (14° potential)
MINIMUM RESIDUAL SUGAR	100 grams
Grape Varieties	
GRENACHE NOIR	{ minimum 50 per cent minimum 75 per cent for Grand Cru

GRENACHE NOIR	minimum 50 per cent minimum 75 per cent for Grand Cru
GRENACHE GRIS GRENACHE BLANC MALVOISIE MACCABÉO	maximum 50 per cent (maximum 25 per cent for Grand Cru)
MUSCAT BLANC À PETITS GRAINS MUSCAT D'ALEXANDRIE	
CARIGNAN CINSAULT SYRAH	maximum 10 per cent

Maceration on the skins must last for at least five days.
For Grand Cru, the wine must be aged a minimum of thirty months in wood.

'Banyuls resembles port, except that it has a slightly ferruginous taste.' So wrote P. Morton Shand in 1928. Banyuls was in fact much better known in the UK in the eighteenth and nineteenth centuries than it is at the present time. It was renowned for its keeping powers: Jullien wrote that the wines improve in quality for up to thirty years, and can last for as long as fifty years without tiring. In the last century Banyuls was used in most French hospitals as a medicinal wine, and was considered an excellent 'pick-me-up'.

The Banyuls region covers the communes of Banyuls, Cerbère, Port-Vendre and Collioure. Banyuls received its Appellation Contrôlée status in 1936. The schist terraces rise high above the Mediterranean, with vines grown up to 450 metres above sea level. There are often violent spring rains, which can wash the thin slaty soil down the slopes, necessitating back-breaking work for the *vignerons* who must replace soil where necessary and build retaining terraces. Oblique drainage tracts, designed to combat erosion, cross the retaining walls of terraces. They are known as *peo de gall*, or cock's foot, and were invented by the Templars. The heavy rain in spring and autumn is channelled in this way, although the eroded soils still have to be replaced periodically.

Many of the small, steeply terraced vineyards are far from the village, and in former days there were *caves de vinification* in the mountain, where the wine was fermented and then channelled to the ageing caves by a series of pottery pipe canals. These can still be seen in places, but they are no longer used.

Although the maximum yield for the appellation is 30 hectolitres per hectare, many producers have much lower yields. The terrain is steeply terraced, with thin topsoil and little moisture during the growing season, giving small yields of around 16-20 hectolitres per hectare in many sites, with only around 8-10 hectolitres in some vintages.

A regional peculiarity is *bail à complant*, where the land is rented out: the hirer owns the vines and bears all the charges, giving a fifth of the crop to the owner by way of rent. The right to rent can be passed on to descendants. About half of the vineyard land in Banyuls is rented in this way.

There are around 1,600 growers, with an average of 1.5 hectares per grower. For most, the vines are a second occupation. In the past the main occupation was fishing and anchovy preservation, but now it is more likely to be tourism.

In the 1940s the ratio of wine produced by co-operatives to that of individual producers was two to one in favour of co-operatives. It is still roughly the same, with four co-operatives: the Groupement Interproducteur du Cru Banyuls, La Banyulencque, L'Étoile, and Les Vignerons de Banyuls. There are also some forty private producers.

The wines vary from young, peppery fruity reds that are bottled young, through to golden tawny wines that are bottled after many years' ageing. There is also one producer making white Banyuls. The term *rancio* may be added to wines that have acquired a certain almost maderized flavour. *Rancio* is a matter of taste, achieved through ageing or soil conditions, or through a combination of the two. It does not have any further legal definition, and is a matter of each grower's tastes. Grand Cru wine has to undergo a second tasting before receiving its *agrément*, or appellation papers; it must also contain a higher percentage of Grenache, and be aged in wood for at least thirty months. Wines that have been bottled young are often designated by the English word vintage, presumably in homage to vintage port. Another word used for this style is *rimage*. Young bottled Banyuls has a rich flavour of cherries and plums, with a peppery tannin and bite. It goes well with cheeses, especially with blue cheeses such as Roquefort, and is also good with chocolate. Wines that have been aged for longer in wood may be described as 5 Ans, 8 Ans, 15 Ans, or may just be vintage-dated. These wines will be mellower and gentler in style, more tawny-coloured, with a softer flavour of toffee and almonds. Most producers make a range of styles, and the sheer volume available can be very confusing.

Most wines are sold with a stopper cork or a screw top, and are considered to be ready to drink on purchase, but one or two producers bottle wines with a long driven cork, for longer ageing and for maturation in bottle. Prices are generally between 30 and 70 francs a bottle at the cellar door, depending on the age of the wine. Quality and style are quite varied, and some very fine old wines are still available.

Domaine de Valcros, Robert Doutres – Robert Doutres is the wine-maker with Château de Jau (Côtes du Roussillon Villages), and the wine is made along traditional lines, with two to three years' ageing in wood. It is a mellow, spicy, gentle style, which can age well in bottle.

L'Étoile – this co-operative offers one of the largest and most confusing ranges.

There are some fifteen to twenty *cuvées* to choose from, back to vintages such as 1967 and 1970, and including some Grand Cru. The aged wines are soft, sweet and toffee-flavoured, with hints of demerara sugar, almost reminiscent of good Marsala. Their 1970 is particularly fine. L'Étoile is one of the few producers who still have wine maturing in *bonbonnes* on terraces in the sun, and their wines are among the best traditional Banyuls. Their cellars in the heart of Banyuls-sur-Mer are worth visiting both for the charming welcome and for the range of wines available to taste.

Domaine du Mas Blanc, Dr Parcé – the most expensive, and almost certainly the finest producer in the region. His wood-aged wines are released after many years, and are superb. His 1967 Banyuls Vieilles Vignes, tasted recently, had a very deep tawny colour, with an attractive mature bouquet of rich, intense peppery fruit. His wines are drier on the palate than many, with very powerful massive baked fruit, and excellent balance.

Domaine de la Rectorie, Parcé Frères – a fairly recent domaine, managed by a group of enthusiasts who have purchased or inherited about 20 hectares of vineyard land and are making serious wines, generally intended for ageing. All their wines are bottled with driven corks, rather than stopper corks, and the wines are generally bottled around four months after the vintage. In addition to Grenache Noir, Gris and Blanc, they have some very old Cinsault vines, which are used in both their Collioure and their Banyuls, and which produce a natural potential alcohol of over 14°, with a very small *rendement*. Planting is at a density of 8,000 vines per hectare (1.25 metres square), which at an average *rendement* of 20 hectolitres per hectare gives about one glass of wine per vine per year! Their Cuvée Parcé Frères is the usual *cuvée* produced in most years, while Cuvée Petra Campadieu is from older vines, later-picked, and made only in the best vintages. Another experiment is Cuvée Léon Parcé aged for a short time in new oak *barriques*, with a softer, toastier flavour that is very unusual for this appellation. It is early days to know how well these wines will age, but the domaine has great potential.

H. Sole – good medium-weight fruity wines, under the description Macéré 2 Ans. Good length, with soft, slightly raisiny/grape sugar finish, and delicate fruit flavours.

Cellier des Templiers – this company markets a range of wines, including some Grand Cru, and some excellent *cuvées* of older wines. Prices are on the high side, but the wines are of good quality.

Vial-Sapéras – an excellent *rancio* wine sold under the Al Tragou label, and the only white Banyuls to be produced. Al Tragou is aged for many years in large oak casks, with an air-gap in the cask allowing gentle oxidation. Lovely intense almost mocha-flavoured wine for the end of a meal. The white, from 60 per cent Grenache Blanc and 40 per cent Grenache Gris, is a new departure. (Apparently the appellation does not specifically mention that the wine should be vinified as a red, although there should be a minimum percentage of Grenache Noir.) Fermentation is carried out at a low temperature, and the wine is aged for two months in new oak *barriques* and is bottled within six to eight months of the vintage. This is more an aperitif style of wine, but would also be excellent with *foie gras* or with lighter desserts. Only around 375 cases are produced each year.

Grand Roussillon, AOC, Vin Doux Naturel

Factfinder	
STATUS	AOC, VDN
COLOUR	Red, white and tawny
SIZE OF REGION	25,000 hectares
AVERAGE ANNUAL PRODUCTION	25 hectolitres red, 5 hectolitres white
MAXIMUM YIELD	30 hectolitres per hectare
MINIMUM ACTUAL ALCOHOL	15°
MAXIMUM ACTUAL ALCOHOL	18°
MINIMUM POTENTIAL ALCOHOL	21.5°
MINIMUM SUGAR AT HARVEST	252 grams per litre (14° potential)
MINIMUM RESIDUAL SUGAR	100 grams
Grape Varieties	
GRENACHE NOIR GRENACHE GRIS GRENACHE BLANC MALVOISIE MACCABÉO MUSCAT BLANC À PETITS GRAINS MUSCAT D'ALEXANDRIE	minimum 90 per cent
CARIGNAN BLANQUETTE ALICANTE MADÈRE	maximum 10 per cent

This appellation can theoretically be used for wines from the regions of Banyuls, Maury and Rivesaltes, but not much is actually declared under this designation. Grand Roussillon can also have the designation *rancio*. As well as Vin Doux Naturel, the appellation also covers *vins de liqueur*, which have no minimum must weight, and which can have over 10 per cent neutral alcohol added.

Grand Roussillon was popular in England in the last century as a potential rival for port, on account of its alcoholic strength, 'which it was fondly imagined was *naturally* as high as 27°', according to P. Morton Shand. The wine of Masdeu, a farm between

Collioure and Port Vendres, was especially in demand, 1,648 hogsheads of it being imported by one London wine merchant in the year 1836-7.

Wines with this appellation are most likely from the older co-operatives, but the name has been largely abandoned. Prices are around 30 francs at the cellar door.

Victor Anthérieu – quite attractive soft fruity wines with wonderful 1920s labels, under the brand names Ransbord and Moskinor.

Maury, AOC, Vin Doux Naturel

Factfinder	
STATUS	AOC, VDN
COLOUR	Red, white and tawny
SIZE OF REGION	2,000 hectares
AVERAGE ANNUAL PRODUCTION	39,300 hectolitres red
	350 hectolitres white
MAXIMUM YIELD	30 hectolitres per hectare
MINIMUM ACTUAL ALCOHOL	15°
MAXIMUM ACTUAL ALCOHOL	18°
MINIMUM POTENTIAL ALCOHOL	21.5°
MINIMUM SUGAR AT HARVEST	252 grams per litre (14° potential)
MINIMUM RESIDUAL SUGAR	100 grams
Grape Varieties	
GRENACHE NOIR	minimum 50 per cent
GRENACHE GRIS	
GRENACHE BLANC	
MALVOISIE	
MACCABÉO	
MUSCAT BLANC À PETITS GRAINS	
MUSCAT D'ALEXANDRIE	
CARIGNAN	
CINSAULT	maximum 10 per cent
SYRAH	
LISTAN	

The Maury appellation covers wines from the communes of Maury, Tautavel, St-

Paul-de-Fenouillet, Rasiguères and Lesquerde, along the banks of the Agly river, north of Perpignan. The soil is principally decomposed black slate, with some gneiss and granite around Lesquerde. Although the minimum *rendement* is 30 hectolitres per hectare, the yield is often down to between 14 and 25 hectolitres. Maury was granted its AC in 1972.

There are three co-operatives producing about 90 per cent of the appellation, and about twelve independent producers. Most of the producers vinify table wine as well as Vin Doux Naturel. Like Banyuls, Maury can be bottled in its youth, when it is often called Vintage, or can be aged in *bonbonne* or cask, when it takes on a tawny colour and is usually sold either by vintage or by number of years in cask. Maury can be labelled *rancio*, where the wine has an aged, almost Madeira-like taste. About one third of Maury is muted 'on the *marc*', and is wine intended for long ageing. Prices range from about 30 francs for a younger wine to 60 or 70 francs for an older vintage.

Mas Amiel – the largest domaine, founded in 1818, and bottling their own wine since 1925. The domaine covers 132 hectares, producing nothing but Maury, from 80 per cent Grenache, and 20 per cent mixed varieties, mainly Cinsault. This is a traditional domaine, with one of the largest parks of glass *bonbonnes*, which are left outside in the heat of the summer and the cold of the winter. After a year in glass, the wines are aged further in old oak casks. The domaine has also started producing a Vintage, which is bottled as soon as possible after fermentation and is young and fruity, with appealing ripe cherry and raspberry flavours. The wine-maker is also experimenting with ageing the wine in new oak *barriques*, for a mellow oaky-flavoured style. The traditional wines are bottled after six, eleven or fifteen years, the older wines taking on a caramel flavour with a hint of volatility, and mellow nutty mature fruit on the palate, with a certain dryness underlying the rich toffee raisin-like sweetness. As well as their commercially available wines, Mas Amiel have small stocks of older single-vintage wines, which have been matured in the traditional way (*bonbonnes* followed by large old oak casks) and are kept for special events or presentations. The 1949 had an old gold, tawny colour, a soft, mellow toffee nose, with a touch of volatility, and complex, woody fruit nuances. The palate was very rich and intense, mellow and elegant, with a certain dryness on the finish, in some aspects like an old *oloroso* sherry. These are certainly wines with superb ageing abilities.

Jean Louis Lafage – one of the smaller domaines, with a shop in the village of Maury. Lafarge produce three *cuvées*, from a young Tradition, through a Rancio, to an older Prestige. The Prestige is far the best, with superb soft ripe black cherry and prune flavours, and excellent length.

Les Vignerons de Maury – this co-operative produces an excellent range of wines, marred only by their rather bright, dumpy-bottled presentation. The top of the range is their Cuvée Chabert de Barbera 1974, in a black frosted bottle. This wine has a soft fruit flavour, reminiscent of prunes and apricots, with excellent length and a nutty finish.

Rivesaltes, AOC, Vin Doux Naturel

Factfinder	
STATUS	AOC, VDN
COLOUR	Red, white and tawny
SIZE OF REGION	20,000 hectares
AVERAGE ANNUAL PRODUCTION	70,500 hectolitres red
	220,000 hectolitres white
MAXIMUM YIELD	30 hectolitres per hectare
MINIMUM ACTUAL ALCOHOL	$15°$
MAXIMUM ACTUAL ALCOHOL	$18°$
MINIMUM POTENTIAL ALCOHOL	$21.5°$
MINIMUM SUGAR AT HARVEST	252 grams per litre ($14°$ potential)
MINIMUM RESIDUAL SUGAR	100 grams
Grape Varieties	
GRENACHE NOIR	minimum 50 per cent for reds
GRENACHE GRIS	
GRENACHE BLANC	
MALVOISIE	maximum 50 per cent for reds,
MACCABÉO	no limit for whites
MUSCAT BLANC À PETITS GRAINS	
MUSCAT D'ALEXANDRIE	
CARIGNAN	
CINSAULT	
SYRAH	maximum 10 per cent
LISTAN	

Rivesaltes was granted its appellation in 1972. It is the largest appellation for Vins Doux Naturels, covering eighty-six communes in Pyrénées-Orientales and six in Aude. It is also the most split-up of the Vins Doux Naturels, with the largest number of growers. There are some sixty-one co-operatives producing Rivesaltes, as well as over 600 independent producers. Wines can be red, tawny, golden, amber or pale gold in colour, and may be young and fruity, or older and softer. Styles, quality, and prices vary tremendously. Although the consumer recognizes the appellation Muscat de Rivesaltes, the plain appellation Rivesaltes is often overlooked. Some of the whites from varieties other than Muscat can be superb. The reds and most old tawnies should be served at room temperature, and the whites lightly chilled. Some of the lighter tawnies are delicious at a cooler temperature, too. In France most of these wines are drunk as aperitifs, but they have plenty of other uses. Reds and tawnies are excellent with cheeses and desserts, and will even stand up to chocolate. They could also be served with richer meat dishes, and are excellent with duck or game. Whites are very good with *foie gras* and *charcuterie*, and some will also be excellent for desserts.

Some bargains can be found in this appellation; wines with twenty to thirty years' age, at very good prices. They are generally less sought after than Maury or Banyuls, and many of the domaines are off the normal tourist path. Thus they are often worth the detour. Prices will vary from about 25-75 francs a bottle at the cellar door.

As with Banyuls and Maury, the wines can be bottled in their youth, and are often labelled Vintage or Rimage. They may be aged, and sold either with the number of years' ageing, or with the vintage date. They can also be labelled *rancio*, often when they have been aged in glass *bonbonnes*, known locally as *touries*, exposed to the sun. Many domaines offer a large range of styles.

Domaine Brial, Cave des Vignerons de Baixas – this excellent co-operative produces both red and white Rivesaltes under the Domaine Brial label. Lovely wood-aged wines, the white being particularly fine.

Domaine Cazes, Rivesaltes – superb tawny-gold Vieux Rivesaltes with gentle buttery mellow nutty flavours, and a hint of perfumed wood-maturation on the finish. Elegant, unassuming but very fine. Prices are increasing for older vintages, but they are still a bargain. They also produce a Vintage style, and a very good matured white under the label Cuvée Aimé Cazes.

Château de Corneilla, Jonquières d'Oriola, Corneilla-del-Vercol – lovely soft tawny-style wines with the same delicate woodiness as an old tawny port. Soft, but with exquisite length of flavour.

Mas de la Garrigue, Marcel Vila, St-Estève – one of the discoveries of the region. Monsieur and Madame Vila have stocks of old Rivesaltes back to 1959. Wines are aged in large, lined concrete tanks, and are predominantly from Grenache Noir. The wines have a deep tawny brown colour, a mellow toffee caramel nose, and sweet grapey soft toffee fruit on the palate.

R. Mounié et Ses Filles, Tautavel – another bargain is Monsieur Mounié's thirty-year-old Nectar du Prieuré, vinified from Grenache Blanc, and from a single vintage, 1955 at present. Rich golden tawny-coloured wine, with buttery toffee-fudge nose and palate, and delicate buttery nutty mature fruit flavours. Superb wines, worth seeking out.

Château de Nouvelles, Robert Daurat-Fort, Tuchan – a domaine producing traditionally aged reds, with *rancio* overtones. Soft, toffee and burnt caramel flavours, with a hint of spice.

Muscat de Rivesaltes, AOC, Vin Doux Naturel

Factfinder	
STATUS	AOC, VDN
COLOUR	White
SIZE OF REGION	24,000 hectares
AVERAGE ANNUAL PRODUCTION	85,000 hectolitres
MAXIMUM YIELD	30 hectolitres per hectare
MINIMUM ACTUAL ALCOHOL	$15°$
MAXIMUM ACTUAL ALCOHOL	$18°$
MINIMUM POTENTIAL ALCOHOL	$21.5°$
MINIMUM SUGAR AT HARVEST	252 grams per litre ($14°$ potential)
MINIMUM RESIDUAL SUGAR	100 grams

Grape Varieties	
MUSCAT BLANC À PETITS GRAINS	minimum 50 per cent
MUSCAT D'ALEXANDRIE	maximum 50 per cent

Muscat de Rivesaltes accounts for some 70 per cent of French Muscat Vin Doux Naturel. The appellation covers ninety communes in the *département* of Pyrénées-Orientales, and nine in Aude, covering the same area as the appellation Rivesaltes, with the exception of the Banyuls area.

All the Vin Doux Naturel Muscat appellations have much in common, coming from the same grapes, with the same method of production. There are more variations between growers than between appellations, although until the last century there was probably more variation to be found, as wine-making methods were less proscribed. Rivesaltes was always one of the most highly regarded Muscat wines, having been produced since Roman times. Its average yield is also one of the lowest, at around 22 hectolitres per hectare, as many of the vineyards are on steep terraces and on thin soils.

Some producers are experimenting with skin contact, leaving the skins in contact with the fermenting grape juice rather than crushing the grapes and fermenting the clear juice. The skins give a more pronounced flavour, but also give a deeper colour, and the process can be more risky. Alcohol can be added before or after the skins are removed from the fermenting juice. Producers may also vary in the percentage of the two Muscat varieties grown, Petits Grains giving more aroma, and Alexandrie a softer, sweeter flavour. The exact point at which alcohol is added will also affect the finished sweetness of the wine. Although in theory the finished alcohol can be anywhere between $15°$ and $18°$, in practice it will always be just over $15°$, as a higher alcohol level would overpower the delicate fruit flavours.

Some wines are lighter and more floral in style; these are excellent as an aperitif, or could even accompany such dishes as asparagus or *foie gras*. Others are fuller and fatter, with a broader, raisiny flavour, and are better suited to desserts. As Muscat does not have much acidity, it is better with fruits that are not too high in acidity, otherwise it can taste a little bland. Prices are generally around 25-30 francs a bottle at the cellar door.

Aphrodis, SIVIR, Banyuls-sur-Mer – one of the largest ranges of Vins Doux Naturels is produced by the Templiers company in Banyuls. It includes three Muscats de Rivesaltes, and these are the wines you are likely to find in the supermarkets, under the trade names Aphrodis, Aliza and Château de Calce. Pleasant but rather anonymous commercial wines in a slightly blowsy style.

Bobé, R. Vila, St-Estève – the brother of Marcel Vila at Mas de la Garrigue produces a light, floral grapey Muscat that is excellent as an aperitif.

Domaine Boudau, Rivesaltes – light style of Muscat which needs to be drunk in its youth. Pleasant, but rather neutral.

Domaine Brial, SCV des Vignerons de Baixas – sweeter, full-flavoured style, with a delicate floral grapey nose, and lovely length of flavour. Clean and very well made.

Château Cap de Fouste, Vignerons Catalans, Perpignan – this *négociant* wine has a rather harsh, almost cheesy style. Not recommended.

Domaine Cazes, Rivesaltes – consistently one of the best Muscats produced, with delicate floral Muscat fruit, excellent length and balance. Their wine is produced partially by skin contact, and with a larger percentage of Alexandrie than usual. Top quality.

Jean d'Estavel, Perpignan – this *négociant* wine is sweet and gentle, lightweight but very charming.

Cave des Producteurs de Fitou, Fitou – a slightly drier, heavier style, less floral but with an attractive grapiness.

Mas de la Garrigue, Marcel Vila, St-Estève – Monsieur Vila's Muscat is made in an old-fashioned style, and is yellower and fatter in flavour, with less floral overtones, but more buttery ripe Muscat flavours. Attractive and unusual.

Henriques, Perpignan – this *négociant*'s Muscat des Abeilles is made in a full-flavoured, raisiny style, with a good weight of fruit. His Domaine de Forca Real is less satisfactory.

Château de Jau, Cases de Pène – fat raisiny muscatel fruit, made as they describe it 'more in a wine style than as an aperitif'. A little drier than many, with good length.

Domaine de Lacroix, SICA Les Vignerons de Rivesaltes, Rivesaltes – a sweeter, more syrupy style, with a ripe fat raisiny flavour. Attractive rich style, made from a higher percentage of Alexandrie than usual. This co-operative's wines may be found under a variety of names, including La Roussillonnaise and Arnaud de Villeneuve.

Ets. Limouzy, Rivesaltes – maybe I had a poor bottle of this wine, but I found it rather dull and almondy, with less Muscat flavour. Unexciting.

Les Producteurs de Mont Tauch, Tuchan – lovely round grapey wine with plenty of Muscat flavour, fresh, floral and very attractive.

Château de Nouvelles, Robert Daurat-Fort, Tuchan – lively fresh grapey Muscat, lightweight and elegant, a good aperitif style.

Domaine Sarda-Malet, Perpignan – unusual wine, with a drier style, and a floral and slightly ginger flavour. Well made: a good aperitif wine.

Les Maîtres Vignerons de Tautavel – attractive rich raisiny Muscat, with fat ripe fruit flavours, and a soft, sweet finish. Well made.

Château de la Tuilerie, Nîmes – why a domaine in Languedoc should offer a Muscat de Rivesaltes in their range is somewhat of a mystery, especially as there are a number of Muscat appellations nearer home to choose from. However, their Muscat is floral and elegant, with aromatic fresh grapey flavours, and is very well made. It is vinified for them by Domaine Cazes.

Muscat de Frontignan, AOC, Vin Doux Naturel

Factfinder	
STATUS	AOC, VDN
COLOUR	White
SIZE OF REGION	750 hectares
AVERAGE ANNUAL PRODUCTION	18,000 hectolitres
MAXIMUM YIELD	40 hectolitres per hectare
MINIMUM ACTUAL ALCOHOL	$15°$
MAXIMUM ACTUAL ALCOHOL	$18°$
MINIMUM POTENTIAL ALCOHOL	$21.9°$
MINIMUM SUGAR AT HARVEST	252 grams per litre ($14°$ potential)
MINIMUM RESIDUAL SUGAR	125 grams
Grape Varieties	
MUSCAT BLANC À PETITS GRAINS	100 per cent

Muscat de Frontignan was granted its appellation in 1936 and has always been one of France's most highly regarded Muscats, coming from vines grown in the communes of Frontignan and Vic-la-Gardiole. The wines were praised by Rabelais, and Jullien stated that it was France's best Muscat after Rivesaltes. It is also claimed that the Marquis de Lur-Saluces visited Frontignan in the 1700s to study the way the wines were made. He then returned to Château d'Yquem, and although he planted different grapes because of the different climate, was modelling his wine on what he had learned in Frontignan.

The wine can also be called Frontignan or Vin de Frontignan. The town of Frontignan bristles with producers' signs, and the wines can be bought in a variety of tasteful bottles made especially for the tourists, in shapes as diverse as a bunch of grapes, a flamenco dancer, or a fist clutching a gun. As well as the co-operatives, which vinify 75 per cent of the production, there are a number of individual producers. Many producers have several wines, and Frontignan produces a *vin doux de liqueur* as well as Vin Doux Naturel. Both may have the same name on the bottle, both are Appellation Contrôlée, and the customer needs to read the small print to tell one from the other. Some producers also vinify a Muscat *naturellement doux*, from late-picked grapes, and occasionally a *mistelle*, with 15° alcohol added before any fermentation. Some of the non-appellation Muscats may have longer ageing in wood, and take on a softer toffee flavour. There is also an *eau-de-vie de Muscat de Frontignan* produced by the co-operative, which is excellent, with a lovely perfumed Muscat grape smell.

The appellation wines may be light and fragrant aperitif-style wines, or may be softer, sweeter and more raisiny. As with all Muscat Vin Doux Naturels, styles vary slightly from one producer to another, as much as from one appellation to another, but Frontignan is considered to be a little fatter in style than most.

Prices are generally between 25 and 35 francs a bottle, and cheaper for the non-appellation wines.

Favier-Bel – very traditional producers making excellent fat, fruity wines, a little softer and more golden than most. They also produce a Muscat Vieux, and another *cuvée* named Raid-Man, both of which have had longer ageing in wood and have a softer, more caramelized flavour.

Cave Co-opérative de Frontignan – ripe grapey Muscat with soft fruit flavours. Attractive and well made.

Château de la Peyrade, Yves Pastourel – lovely soft full-flavoured Muscat, with rich, raisiny, honeyed fruit flavours.

Château de Stony – attractive quite lightweight wine, with soft grapey ripe fruit. Nicely made.

Muscat de Lunel, AOC, Vin Doux Naturel

Factfinder	
STATUS	AOC, VDN
COLOUR	White
SIZE OF REGION	185 hectares
AVERAGE ANNUAL PRODUCTION	9,000 hectolitres
MAXIMUM YIELD	40 hectolitres per hectare
MINIMUM ACTUAL ALCOHOL	$15°$
MAXIMUM ACTUAL ALCOHOL	$18°$
MINIMUM POTENTIAL ALCOHOL	$21.9°$
MINIMUM SUGAR AT HARVEST	252 grams per litre ($14°$ potential)
MINIMUM RESIDUAL SUGAR	125 grams
Grape Varieties	
MUSCAT BLANC À PETITS GRAINS 100 per cent	

Muscat de Lunel is produced from vines grown on limestone terraces in the communes of Lunel, Lunel-Vieil, Vérargues and Saturargues, to the east of Montpellier. The region was granted its appellation in 1943, and has a long history of fine Muscat production. The region also used to produce *eau-de-vie* from red grapes.

The story goes that in 1730 the Abbot Bouquet owned a vineyard called the Côte du Mazet in Lunel-Vieil. His Muscat was of outstanding quality, known throughout France and abroad, and he was thought to have a secret recipe, which all the other growers coveted. When he died in 1780, his recipe was found among his papers: '*Maturité et propreté, voilà tout mon secret pour faire un excellent vin muscat*' (Ripeness and good hygiene, that is all the secret needed to produce an excellent Muscat). A Monsieur Gauthier bought the vineyard after the abbot's death, and increased the area of vines. He picked the grapes using several passages through the vineyard, choosing only the ripest grapes each time, and his wine was reputed to age very well.

The area is less beautiful now than it must have been in those days. The motorway from Montpellier to Nîmes runs past the vineyards, and the area is rather industrial. Apart from the co-operative, there are few wine producers to be seen without searching hard.

The wine is reputed to have less body than Frontignan, and to be more forward in style, but once again the styles produced are quite varied from one producer to the next. Prices are around 30-40 francs a bottle at the cellar door.

Domaine de Bellevue, Francis Lacoste – fairly new domaine producing big, broad ripe Muscat wines in a softer, more forward style.

Château du Grès Saint-Paul – good-quality wines from this small producer. Floral elegant wines with strong Muscat aromas and flavours.

Cave du Muscat de Lunel – the co-operative produces several styles, the best being labelled Château de la Tour de Farges. Their wines are quite delicate in style, with floral grapey flavours, very attractive.

Muscat de Mireval, AOC, Vin Doux Naturel

Factfinder	
STATUS	AOC, VDN
COLOUR	White
SIZE OF REGION	150 hectares
AVERAGE ANNUAL PRODUCTION	6,500 hectolitres
MAXIMUM YIELD	40 hectolitres per hectare
MINIMUM ACTUAL ALCOHOL	$15°$
MAXIMUM ACTUAL ALCOHOL	$18°$
MINIMUM POTENTIAL ALCOHOL	$21.9°$
MINIMUM SUGAR AT HARVEST	252 grams per litre ($14°$ potential)
MINIMUM RESIDUAL SUGAR	125 grams
Grape Varieties	
MUSCAT BLANC À PETITS GRAINS	100 per cent

Mireval is a small appellation, with vines grown on stony limestone soils between Frontignan and the village of Mireval, to the south of the Gardiole *massif*. The wines are often sweeter in style, more raisiny and fatter than many other Muscats, with a pronounced floral bouquet. Production is limited to two co-operatives and about a dozen private producers. Prices are generally between 30 and 35 francs a bottle at the cellar door.

Domaine de la Capelle, J. Maraval – this domaine produces two *cuvées*, a Traditional and a Sélectionnée, and their wines are highly perfumed and aromatic in style, with rich Muscat flavours.

Domaine du Mas Neuf – elegant grapey floral wines with medium weight. Good aperitif style.

Domaine de Moulinas, Monsieur Aymas – lighter wine, with attractive floral grapey flavours, and a gentler weight of fruit. Good aperitif style.

Mas du Pigeonnier – small domaine producing excellent ripe honeyed fat Muscat-flavoured wines, with good length. Rich and well balanced.

Cave Rabelais – this co-operative produces good-quality wines, with ripe raisiny honeyed flavours, always very reliable.

Muscat de Saint-Jean de Minervois AOC, Vin Doux Naturel

Factfinder	
STATUS	AOC, VDN
COLOUR	White
SIZE OF REGION	50 hectares
AVERAGE ANNUAL PRODUCTION	1,900 hectolitres
MAXIMUM YIELD	40 hectolitres per hectare
MINIMUM ACTUAL ALCOHOL	15°
MAXIMUM ACTUAL ALCOHOL	18°
MINIMUM POTENTIAL ALCOHOL	21.5°
MINIMUM SUGAR AT HARVEST	252 grams per litre (14° potential)
MINIMUM RESIDUAL SUGAR	100 grams
Grape Varieties	
MUSCAT BLANC À PETITS GRAINS	100 per cent

The commune of St-Jean-de-Minervois is at an altitude of 250-300 metres, on the border of a limestone plateau, with topsoils of stony slate. Because of the higher altitude, picking is usually three to four weeks later than for the other Muscat appellations, and this is the only commune in the region growing Muscat. It is a very pretty little hill village, surrounded by vineyards, and at this altitude the other vineyards of the Minervois have almost been left behind.

St-Jean-de-Minervois has a long history of Muscat production, and was granted its appellation in 1972, after having been delimited in 1949. This is the smallest appellation for Muscat, most of which is produced by the co-operative, with only a handful of other producers. The wines are delicate in style, with a pronounced floral bouquet. They are generally lighter in weight than the other VDN Muscats. Prices are around 35-40 francs a bottle at the cellar door.

Domaine de Barroubio, Mme Miquel – delightful perfumed grapey Muscat, lightweight and very attractive. Good aperitif style.
Domaine Simon, H. Simon – lovely aromatic floral Muscat, with delicate light fruit and plenty of finesse.

Vins de Pays

The current legislation for Vins de Pays was laid down in 1979, although the idea is an old one. In the 1930s wines could be designated '*vin de pays du canton de . . .*', but this was a purely regional designation which did not take quality into consideration. After Algeria's independence the French wine-makers wanted to set up specific area names to guarantee authenticity and origin, and to encourage quality wine production. Now Vin de Pays is an official denomination, controlling not just the area of production, but specifying yields, recommended varieties, minimum ripeness of grapes, and incorporating an official analysis and tasting. Vins de Pays are table wines from a specific region, or 'the élite of the *vins de table*'. The region designated may be very large, or may cover a single village.

Vins de Pays are less restricted than Appellation Contrôlée in permitted varieties, and allow the producer to experiment more, and to produce a more individual wine according to his personal taste.

Total *rendement*, or yield, is limited to a maximum of 100 hectolitres per hectare, and in many cases to 70 or 80 hectolitres. This may seem quite high, but many of the basic table wine vineyards in Languedoc-Roussillon can achieve yields of up to 250 hectolitres! There is certainly no lack of sun to ripen the grapes in southern France; the limiting factors are water and nutrient availability. Some high-quality wines can be produced with these permitted yields.

Grape varieties for Vins de Pays within Languedoc-Roussillon usually include the ubiquitous Cinsault, Carignan and Grenache for the reds and rosés, with increasing additions of Syrah, Cabernet Sauvignon, Cabernet Franc, Merlot, and Mourvèdre. For whites, the traditional Ugni Blanc, Clairette, Terret and Maccabéo are often joined by Chardonnay and Sauvignon. Some of the Vin de Pays designations may be rather vague, laying down that the wines must come from *cépages recommandés*, while other regions are more specific.

The minimum natural alcohol is generally 10° for Languedoc-Roussillon, with certain designations specifying a higher degree. The wines of this area cannot be chaptalized.

Unlike unidentified table wines, Vins de Pays can use the terms 'Mont', 'Côte', 'Coteaux', or 'Val' to designate the zone of production, and 'Domaine' or 'Mas' to designate the name of the property producing the wine. (They cannot, however, use 'Château'.) They can specify the vintage and the grape variety used. In theory a Vin de Pays regions could be upgraded to VDQS or even to AOC if the quality warranted the promotion.

More and more wines are being vinified as 'varietals', wines sold as a single grape variety. These are certainly easier for the consumer to remember than the different Vin de Pays designations, which number well over 100 in the Languedoc-Roussillon area.

The vast majority of Vins de Pays are produced by co-operatives, which have often been instrumental in forming the various designations, and may account for the entire production in some of the smaller ones. Many Vins de Pays are also blended and marketed by large *négociant* companies which provide the supermarket and hypermarket chains with 'generic' or 'own label' wines. Much of this wine is sold as a non-vintage style, blended to provide the same style from year to year, providing wines of good basic quality at a low price. Similarly, many bag-in-the-box and tetrabriks, or cartons of wine, will be Vins de Pays.

There are also Vins de Pays at the more expensive end of the scale from both co-operatives and private estates, often made as special *cuvées*, from more popular and highly regarded varieties, with increasing use of oak for maturation.

Another trend is in *primeur* wines, vinified in the same way as Beaujolais Nouveau and put on the market from October to Christmas in the year of production, often in carafe-type bottles. These ensure a quick turnover and profit for the wine-maker, and provide light, fruity, quaffable wine at a very reasonable price compared with Beaujolais Nouveau.

Demand for white wines is growing. Some of these regions have very little planted in the way of white grapes, and co-operatives have been experimenting with vinifying red grapes off the skins to produce white wine. Recently growers have planted more white varieties, especially Chardonnay, which is always in demand and fetches a good price. Sauvignon plantings are increasing too, and growers are also experimenting with Viognier. The traditional white varieties are being vinified by modern methods to give a fresher style of wine. Grapes are picked a little earlier to retain their acidity, and are vinified at a cooler temperature to retain more aroma and delicacy.

Prices for Vins de Pays are very varied. Many can be purchased for as little as 7-10 francs at the cellar door, although an increasing number of top blends sell for 25 francs or over.

Consumer campaigns both in France and abroad are increasing customer awareness of the Vin de Pays designation, and sales are rising fast in response to increased demand. Production of Vins de Pays is on the increase, from 5,600,000 hectolitres in 1982 to 6,100,000 in 1983, and over 8,000,000 in 1990. Annual figures for any particular Vin de Pays designation may change quite radically, as many regions can choose from a number of designations, as dictated by fashion or market forces.

Some 85 per cent of all Vins de Pays are from the Mediterranean region, with Languedoc-Roussillon accounting for the lion's share.

The Vin de Pays Designation

There are three basic categories of Vin de Pays: regional, departmental and local.

The regional designation covers the largest and most general zone, and can include several *départements*. The whole of France is divided into three. Wines from different areas within a single region may be grouped together under the regional name, allowing large quantities of wine to be commercialized under one name. Many of these wines are found under brand names. The regional designation for Languedoc-Roussillon is Vin de Pays d'Oc.

Vin de Pays d'Oc covers the whole Languedoc-Roussillon and more besides. A Vin de Pays d'Oc can come from anywhere within the *départements* of Aude, Pyrénées-Orientales, Gard or Hérault, which make up the Languedoc-Roussillon region. They can also be produced in part of the *départements* of Ardèche, Bouches-du-Rhône, Var and Vaucluse. They may come from one specific area, or they may be blended from wines from different regions within the overall area.

These wines are often sold under brand names, providing a consistent, inexpensive wine that can be marketed in very large quantities. The Vin de Pays d'Oc region produces over 4,800,000 hectolitres, much of which could be sold under more specific local names. The majority is red, and an increasing amount is sold as single varietal wines. Styles vary tremendously, the overall trend being to move away from the big, peppery, heavy alcoholic wines to lighter, suppler, softer wines.

Departmental and Local Designations

Departmental designations cover the name of the *département* or county in which the wines are produced. If the *département* name is already used for an Appellation Contrôlée wine, as in Savoie or Jura, it cannot also be used for a Vin de Pays. Again, many of these wines are sold under brand names. The departmental designations for Languedoc-Roussillon are Vin de Pays des Pyrénées-Orientales, de l'Aude, du Gard and de l'Hérault.

Local or sub-regional designations may cover a village, or a group of villages, or a specific region within a *département*. These vary in size, and number over 100 in the Languedoc-Roussillon region. They might be more specific as to the character of wine produced than is the case of the larger regions covered by the first two categories. These wines may be a few francs more expensive than wines from the first two categories, but will often be more individual and interesting in character, and will be more likely to include the wines from individual estates. However, the sheer number of names is confusing, and many are unlikely to be met with outside their local area. The system also means that one wine can have the choice of several guises, and may even appear under different designations in different vintages.

Vins de Pays des Pyrénées-Orientales

This designation covers wines from within the Pyrénées-Orientales *département*, which may be blended from several areas or may be from one single grower. The majority is produced by co-operatives, an increasing majority being vinified as *primeur*. About 80 per cent of the production is red, the remainder rosé, with only 1 or

2 per cent white. The total for the *département*, excluding more regional designations, is around 250,000 hectolitres. These wines are among the lighter Vins de Pays for Languedoc-Roussillon. The majority are sold locally. The usual grape mix is Grenache, Cinsault and Carignan, with some areas adding Merlot, Cabernet and Syrah. Whites are from Grenache Blanc and Maccabéo, with Sauvignon and Chardonnay.

Local or sub-regional designations within the Pyrénées-Orientales are:

Origin	*Styles of wine produced*	*Annual production*
Vin de Pays Catalan South and south-west of Perpignan.	Full-flavoured reds, 11.5° and over; some *primeur*, a little rosé and white.	100,000–130,000 hectolitres.
Vin de Pays des Côtes Catalanes Rivesaltes region, also part of the Agly Valley and the top of the Têt Valley.	Red, rosé and a little white. Some *primeur*.	50,000 hectolitres.
Vin de Pays des Coteaux des Fenouillèdes North of Perpignan, slopes of the Agly Valley, seventeen communes.	Mostly red (90 per cent), rosé 8 per cent and a little white.	20,000 hectolitres.
Vin de Pays des Vals d'Agly Upper Agly Valley, around St-Paul-de-Fenouillet, altitude around 250 metres.	Mostly red, minimum 11°, some *primeur*.	15,000 hectolitres.
Vin de Pays de la Côte Vermeille Coastal area, extreme southern tip of French coastline.	Red, white and rosé. Some good wines from Muscat, as well as usual varieties.	200–500 hectolitres.

Some good wines from this *département* are:

Vin de Pays Catalan
Domaine Cazes, Rivesaltes – produces both sweet and dry Muscat wines, with around 12° alcohol. The dry is an excellent aperitif wine, with elegant light floral Muscat flavour.

Vin de Pays des Côtes Catalanes
Domaine Cazes, Rivesaltes – produces a red and a white under the label Le Canon du Maréchal. The red is from a blend of Grenache, Merlot, Syrah and other varieties, vinified partly by *macération carbonique*, and is fresh, light and lively. The white, from Grenache Blanc, Maccabéo, Sauvignon and Chardonnay, is crisp, clean, and surprisingly elegant. Well-made wines.

Vins de Pays de l'Aude

The departmental designation is used for wines which may come from one or more districts within the Aude *département*. The wines cover a large range of styles, and are generally full-flavoured and ripe. The minimum natural alcohol is 11°, and varieties include Carignan, Grenache and Cinsault, Syrah, Merlot and Cabernet, with an overall possibility of some thirty varieties. The total declared under this designation, excluding more regional designations, is around 1,200,000 hectolitres. Some of the more interesting wines from this department are from more recently introduced varietals, such as Merlot and Viognier.

Local or sub-regional designations within the Aude are:

Origin	*Styles of wine produced*	*Annual production*
Vin de pays de la Haute Vallée de l'Aude		
Large area, fifty communes around the region of Limoux, west of Carcassonne.	Mainly reds, often vinified as single varieties, including Cabernet, Merlot. Some white from Mauzac, also Chenin, Chardonnay.	30,000 hectolitres.
Vin de Pays des Côtes de Prouille		
Between Carcassonne, Limoux and Castelnaudary.	60 per cent red, 35 per cent rosé and 5 per cent white. Some vinified as single varieties.	10,000 hectolitres.
Vin de Pays des Côtes de Lastours		
Twenty-one communes in the Cabardès region, overlooked by Montagne Noire.	Distinctive-flavoured reds, with some Cabernet and Merlot as well as local varieties. Some *primeurs*.	12,000 hectolitres.

Vin de Pays de la Cité de Carcassonne

| Eleven communes around the town of Carcassonne. | 75 per cent red, from traditional varieties, including Merlot and Cabernet Sauvignon. | 30,000 hectolitres. |

Vin de Pays des Coteaux de Peyriac

| Centre of Minervois, seventeen communes, 5,000 hectares. Part of this designation is in the Hérault. | 85 per cent red, 12 per cent rosé and a small quantity of white. Increasing use of Merlot, Syrah and Mourvèdre. | 300,000 hectolitres. |

Vin de Pays des Hauts de Badens

| Commune of Badens, south of the Minervois. | Mainly red wines, traditional varieties, with some Syrah. | 5,000 hectolitres. |

Vin de Pays des Coteaux de Miramont

| Nine communes around the village of Capendu, at the foot of the Alaric mountain. | Mainly red, some vinified as *primeur*, and a little rosé. Traditional varieties including Merlot. | 60,000 hectolitres. |

Vin de Pays du Lézignanais

| Twelve communes around the town of Lézignan, between Corbières and Minervois. | Mainly reds (80 per cent), the balance rosé. Some *primeur*. | 20,000–30,000 hectolitres. |

Vin de Pays du Val-de-Cesse

| Hillsides surrounding the Cesse river, south of the Minervois. | Red, rosé and white, traditional varieties with addition of Cabernet and Merlot. | 20,000 hectolitres. |

Vin de Pays du Val d'Orbieu

| Nine communes between Narbonne and Luzignan, named after the Orbieu river. | 66 per cent red, balance rosé. Traditional varieties. Growing *primeur* market. | 45,000 hectolitres. |

Origin	Styles of wine produced	Annual production

Vin de Pays des Coteaux de la Cabrerisse

St-Laurent-de-la-Cabrerisse and two neighbouring communes, Thézan and Monteret.	80 per cent red, balance rosé and a little white. Some *primeur*.	15,000 hectolitres.

Vin de Pays de Cucugnan

Commune of Cucugnan, north-east of Perpignan.	Fruity reds, minimum 11°, a little crisp dry white.	10,000 hectolitres.

Vin de Pays de Hauterive en Pays d'Aude

Nine communes in Corbières region, north, west and south of Narbonne.	Mainly red, from local varieties with additions of Syrah, Merlot and Cabernet. Some *primeur*.	30,000 hectolitres.

Vin de Pays du Val de Dagne

Fourteen communes around Servies-en-Val, south-east of Carcassonne.	Red and rosé, some vinified as *primeur*.	10,000 hectolitres.

Vin de Pays des Coteaux du Termènes

Hillsides to the north of Monthounet, altitude around 600 metres.	Mostly red, some rosé. Often blended with wines of other regions, rather than sold under own identity.	2,000 hectolitres.

Vin de Pays des Coteaux Cathares

Ten communes in Hautes-Corbières, around region of Tuchan-Paziols.	Red and rosé, good proportion of *primeur*.	30,000 hectolitres.

Vin de Pays des Coteaux du Littoral Audois

Slopes bordering the Mediterranean coast between Narbonne and Perpignan.	Mostly red (80 per cent), rosé and whites from local varieties. Wines for drinking in their youth.	20,000–25,000 hectolitres.

Vin de Pays de la Vallée du Paradis

Ten communes in Corbières region, around Durban, Cascastel and Coustouge.	Mainly red, from local varieties. Some *primeur*.	30,000–40,000 hectolitres.

Vin de Pays des Coteaux de Narbonne

Around Narbonne and three neighbouring communes.	Red, rosé and whites from traditional varieties.	15,000 hectolitres.

Vin de Pays des Côtes de Pérignan

South-east of Narbonne, near the coast, excluding La Clape	Red and rosé, a little *primeur*.	20,000 hectolitres.

Some good wines from this department include:

Vin de Pays de l'Aude
Jacques Boyer produces an excellent Viognier under this designation.

Vin de Pays de la Haute Vallée de l'Aude
Marc Ramires, Antugnac – Marc Ramires has plantings of Pinot Noir, Cabernet Sauvignon, Merlot, Syrah and Grenache for his red wine, and Chardonnay and Mauzac for the white. Excellent-quality wines under the label Prieuré d'Antugnac and les Sieurs d'Auriac. These wines need several years' ageing.

Vins de Pays de l'Hérault

Over 1,100,000 hectolitres of Vin de Pays are produced under this designation, mainly from the three traditional varieties, but with increasing quantities of Syrah, Cabernet, Merlot and Mourvèdre. Around 75 per cent is red, with 20 per cent in rosé and a small amount of white. Quality and styles vary tremendously throughout the region, which includes France's most famous, most expensive, and best Vin de Pays: Mas de Daumas Gassac. There are many privately owned domaines in Hérault, and this *département*'s Vins de Pays include most of the best of Languedoc-Roussillon.

Local or sub-regional designations within the Hérault are:

Origin	Styles of wine produced	Annual production
Vin de Pays des Coteaux d'Enserune		
Eleven communes west of Béziers.	Red and rosé wines from traditional varieties, with some Syrah, Cabernet and Merlot.	15,000 hectolitres.
Vin de Pays des Coteaux de Fontcaude		
Six communes west of Béziers, south-east of St-Chinian.	80 per cent reds, the balance rosé. A good proportion made as *primeur*.	23,000 hectolitres.
Vin de Pays des Côtes de Brian		
Fourteen communes, covering 6,500 hectares between Minerve and the Canal du Midi.	Mainly reds, from the traditional varieties with some Syrah. Some *primeur*.	40,000 hectolitres
Vin de Pays des Monts de la Grage		
Hillsides in the St-Chinian region.	Mainly reds, from the traditional varieties with some Syrah.	300–400 hectolitres.
Vin de Pays de Cessenon		
Commune of Cessenon only.	Reds from the traditional varieties.	650 hectolitres.
Vin de Pays des Coteaux de Murviel		
Around the commune of Murviel-les-Béziers, in the valleys of Libron and Orb.	Reds, rosé and whites from traditional varieties, with increasing use of introduced varieties such as Cabernet, Sauvignon Blanc and Merlot.	30,000–45,000 hectolitres.
Vin de Pays des Coteaux de Laurens		
Around the commune of Laurens, near Faugères.	80 per cent reds, the balance rosé from traditional varieties, with some Syrah, and recent plantations of Chardonnay and Pinot Noir.	25,000 hectolitres.

Vin de Pays des Coteaux du Salagou

Twenty communes between the Salagou lake and Lodève.	80 per cent red, the balance rosé, from traditional varieties with additions of Syrah and Mourvèdre.	5,000 hectolitres.

Vin de Pays de la Haute-Vallée de l'Orb

Around Bédarieux, in the upper Orb Valley.	Mainly red wines, from the traditional varieties.	200–400 hectolitres.

Vin de Pays du Mont Baudille

Slopes of the Causses, around St-Jean-de-la-Blaquière.	Mainly red, a little rosé and white, from traditional varieties. Generally unexciting.	13,000–25,000 hectolitres.

Vin de Pays des Gorges de l'Hérault

Three communes around Gignac.	66 per cent red, the balance rosé, from traditional varieties, with the addition of Syrah, Cabernet and Merlot.	8,000 hectolitres.

Vin de Pays du Val de Montferrand

South of Pic St-Loup, around the commune of St-Mathieu-de-Tréviers. Quite high altitudes.	70 per cent red and 20 per cent rosé from traditional varieties, especially Carignan. 10 per cent white, mainly Ugni Blanc. Some *primeur*.	35,000 hectolitres.

Vin de Pays de la Bénovie

Around St-Christol, north of Montpellier.	Mainly red, some rosé from varieties. 5 per cent white from Ugni Blanc.	15,000 hectolitres.

Vin de Pays du Bérange

Region of Castries and Lunel Viel, east of the *département*.	Mainly red, some rosé.	7,000 hectolitres.

Origin	*Styles of wine produced*	*Annual production*
Vin de Pays des Collines de la Moure		
Twenty-seven communes along the hillsides known as Montagne de la Moure, between Montpellier and Sète.	65 per cent red, 30 per cent rosé and 5 per cent white from traditional varieties.	100,000 hectolitres.
Vin de Pays de la Vicomté d'Aumelas		
Thirteen communes on the left bank of the Hérault between Gignac and Montagnac.	85 per cent red and rosé from traditional varieties, with increasing use of Cabernet and Syrah. 15 per cent white, mainly from Ugni Blanc.	20,000 hectolitres.
Vin de Pays des Côtes du Ceressou		
Fifteen communes between Lodève and Béziers.	Red and rosé from traditional varieties, with Syrah, Merlot and Cabernet. 15 per cent white from Ugni, Clairette and Terret. Increasing *primeur* production.	4,000 hectolitres.
Vin de Pays de Caux		
Single commune north-east of Pézenas on the slopes of Cévennes.	Mainly rosé from traditional grapes.	10,000–15,000 hectolitres.
Vin de Pays de Cassan		
Four communes north of Pézenas, around Roujan.	66 per cent red, balance rosé, from traditional varieties.	10,000–15,000 hectolitres.
Vin de Pays de Pézenas		
Commune of Pézenas, on the banks of the Hérault.	Mainly red, from traditional varieties with Cabernet and Merlot. Some *primeur*.	5,500 hectolitres.

Vin de Pays des Côtes de Thongue

Fourteen communes along the Thongue river, north-east of Béziers, 14,000 hectares.

Red and rosé (minimum 11°) from traditional varieties with the addition of Cabernet, Syrah and Merlot. Some good single varietal wines. A little white from Ugni Blanc.

35,000–40,000 hectolitres.

Vin de Pays des Coteaux du Libron

Banks of Libron river, a tributary of the Hérault, north-east of Béziers.

80 per cent red and 20 per cent rosé from traditional varieties with the addition of Cabernet and Merlot. Some *primeur*.

60,000 hectolitres.

Vin de Pays de Bessan

Around the commune of Bessan, north of Agde and south of Pézenas.

60 per cent rosé, 20 per cent red, 20 per cent white, from traditional varieties. Some good *primeur* wines.

5,000–12,000 hectolitres.

Vin de Pays de l'Ardailhou

Tributary between the Hérault and Orb rivers, south of the Hérault *département*.

Red and rosé from traditional varieties.

15,000 hectolitres.

Vin de Pays des Côtes de Thau

North-west of Thau basin, around Florensac, Marseillan, Pomerols and Pinet.

Mainly white, from Carignan Blanc, Terret and Picpoul. Some red from traditional varieties, but the whites are generally more interesting.

60,000 hectolitres.

Vin de Pays des Coteaux de Bessilles

Region on the banks of the Bessilles.

70 per cent red, 20 per cent rosé and 10 per cent white.

12,000 hectolitres.

Some recommended wines from this department are:

Vins de Pays de l'Hérault

Domaine d'Aupilhac, Fadat, Montpeyroux – big, powerful reds from old Carignan vines. Peppery, rustic, gamey style, with tremendous strong flavours and good length. Much more individual in style than most Vins de Pays.

Domaine de Bosc, Pierre Besinet, Vias – one of the finest Sauvignons I have tasted from southern France, with crisp clean aromatic fruit flavours. Not cheap, but still good value. Also an unusual Grenache Blanc, in a gentle peachy style, almost verging on oxidation, but very attractive. The red is well made, with deep ruby colour, attractive quite stalky Cabernet fruit on the palate, and a little astringency.

Domaine de Capion, Philippe Salasc, Gignac – a neighbour of Daumas Gassac. Some of Capion's wines are sold as Vin de Pays d'Oc, and some as Vin de Pays d'Hérault. Attractive well-made wines, improving with each vintage.

Mas de Daumas Gassac, Guibert de la Vaissière, Aniane (see page 143) – the most expensive Vin de Pays in France; reds from a blend, predominantly Cabernet, and whites from Viognier, Chardonnay, Petit Manseng and Muscat. High-quality wines with tremendous ageing potential. Older vintages are often cheaper in the UK than from the domaine.

Domaine la Fadèze, Georges Lenthéric, Marseillan – excellent white from the Terret-Bourret or Terret Gris variety. also an attractive Grenache red, with fresh young raspberry fruit flavours.

Domaine St-Martin, Teisserenc, Pouzolles – the same producers who vinify the Domaine de l'Arjolle wines (see Cotes de Thongue, page 137). An excellent Sauvignon is produced under the St-Martin label, crisp, fresh and very lively.

Domaine St-Martin-de-la-Garrigue, François Henry, Montagnac – lovely smoky spicy Chardonnay, with a hint of oak-ageing, and excellent balance and length. One of the best southern French Chardonnays I have tasted. Also well-made red in two *cuvées*: Bronzinelle, which is soft and brambly, and Reservée, which is more austere and peppery.

Cave Co-opérative La Vigneronne, Pignan – good value range of varietals, including a Cabernet Sauvignon, a Merlot and an excellent Mourvèdre. The non-varietal red and white, although very cheap, are unremarkable.

Vin de Pays des Coteaux de Murviel

Guy and Peyre, Coujan, Murviel – soft, mellow red Vin de Pays from 75 per cent Merlot and 25 per cent Cabernet, as well as ripe soft grapey white from Sauvignon. The red ages extremely well, and the domaine still have small stocks of older vintages, which bear witness to the wine's keeping qualities.

Domaine de Ravanès, Guy Benin, Thezan-les-Béziers (see page 154) – full-bodied powerful reds from Cabernet, Merlot and Petit Verdot, and an excellent white in 1990 from late-picked Ugni Blanc.

Vin de Pays des Coteaux de Laurens

Domaine de la Commanderie de St-Jean, Château de Grézan, Laurens – soft toasty Chardonnay produced by this Faugères estate. A little neutral in its youth, but improves greatly with a year's ageing. The domaine also produce Pinot Noir and Cabernet, but the Chardonnay is the most successful.

Vin de Pays des Collines de la Moure
Domaine de Terre Mégère, Michel Moreau, Cournonsec – soft dry red from the Merlot grape. Gentle, fruity, and well made.

Vin de Pays de la Vicomté d'Aumelas
Aymes, Mireval – attractive lightweight reds from this Muscat de Mireval producer.
Co-opérative de Plaissan – clean lightweight reds with an attractive light elegance.

Vin de Pays des Côtes de Thongue
Domaine du Prieuré d'Amilhac, Régis & Max Cazottes, Servian – very well-made Chardonnay, one of the best from Languedoc-Roussillon. Fermented in new Alliers oak, but without too much oak flavour. Balanced, toasty wines with good varietal character.
Domaine de l'Arjolle, Teisserenc, Pouzolas – a range of well-vinified varietal wines, including Sauvignon, Muscat Sec, and an excellent Cabernet-based red with a hint of new oak and plenty of character.

Vins de Pays du Gard

Some 450,000–500,000 hectolitres per annum are produced under this designation, roughly two-thirds red, the remainder rosé with a small amount of white. A good proportion of the wine is vinified as *primeur*. As usual, most of the wines are made by the co-operatives, but there are several private domaines, especially around Nîmes. Although there are some good Vins de Pays from this *département*, the majority are cheap and cheerful, for drinking as young as possible.

Local or sub-regional designations within the Gard are:

Origin	*Styles of wine produced*	*Annual production*
Vin de Pays de la Vistrenque		
Banks of river Vistre, north-east of the Gard. New designation.	Red and rosé from the traditional varieties.	1,000 hectolitres.
Vin de Pays des Côtes du Vidourle		
Hillsides surrounding the Vidourle Valley, fifteen communes north of Montpellier.	85 per cent red, the balance rosé, from traditional varieties. Some *primeur*.	10,000–15,000 hectolitres.

Origin	*Styles of wine produced*	*Annual production*
Vin de Pays de la Vaunage		
West of Nîmes.	Light reds and rosés from the traditional varieties.	2,000 hectolitres.
Vin de Pays des Coteaux du Salavès		
Hillsides south of Alès, in the region of Sauve, after which it is named.	80 per cent red, the balance rosé, from the traditional varieties with the addition of Syrah, Cabernet and Merlot. Some *primeur*.	15,000 hectolitres.
Vin de Pays du Serre du Coiran		
Foothills of Cévennes between Anduze and Lédignan, south of Alès.	66 per cent red, the balance rosé, from traditional varieties. Some *primeur*.	10,000 hectolitres.
Vin de Pays du Mont Bouquet		
Around the commune of Brouzet-les-Alès, south-east of Alès.	Red and rosé from the traditional varieties, with increasing Cabernet and Merlot. Some *primeur*.	30,000 hectolitres.
Vin de Pays des Coteaux Cévenols		
Foothills of Cévennes, north-east of Alès.	60 per cent red, 40 per cent rosé from the traditional varieties.	5,000 hectolitres.
Vin de Pays des Coteaux de Cèze		
Banks of the river Cèze, which flows into the Rhône. Forty-six communes.	Red and rosé wines from the traditional varieties.	6,000 hectolitres.
Vin de Pays de l'Uzège		
Former duchy of Uzès, in Cévennes. Twenty-seven communes.	70 per cent red and 20 per cent rosé from traditional varieties, mainly Grenache.	15,000 hectolitres.

Vin de Pays des Coteaux du Pont du Gard

| Nineteen communes in the region of Pont du Gard, centring on Rémoulins. | Mainly reds, from traditional varieties with a little Syrah. Some *primeur*. | 50,000 hectolitres. |

Vin de Pays des Coteaux Flaviens

| Part of Costières du Gard, between Beaucaire and Vauvert. | Mainly reds, from the traditional varieties with some Syrah. Some whites from Ugni Blanc and Grenache Blanc. | 35,000 hectolitres. |

Vin de Pays des Côtes de Libac

| Between Anduze and Lédignan, south of Alès. | Mainly reds, from traditional varieties. | 3,000 hectolitres. |

Vin de Pays des Sables du Golfe du Lion

| Sand dunes along the coast of Hérault and Gard, up to the Rhône estuary. | 20 per cent red, 55 per cent rosé and 25 per cent white, from a large range of varieties. Light rosé or gris is a speciality. Some very well-made wines. | 150,000–160,000 hectolitres. |

Some of the best wines from the Gard department include:

Vin de Pays des Sables du Golfe du Lion

Listel, Salins du Midi – the largest wine estate in France, owning 1,700 hectares of vines along the coastal region. Reds are from Carignan, Cabernet, Syrah, Grenache, and Merlot, which are also used for the rosé wines. Much of the rosé is produced as a very light *gris* style, popular locally, where it is excellent with local fish and shellfish dishes. Whites are from Ugni Blanc, Clairette and Sauvignon. Whites and rosés are sometimes produced *sur lie*, which indicates that they have spent the winter in the casks or tanks on the lees of fermentation, and have been bottled straight from those lees, giving a slight 'spritz' to the flavour, and a little more weight. Excellent quality wines, very reliable.

Sabledoc – the other main group producing this appellation, often under a large number of individual property names. Pleasant, light, inexpensive wines.

All of the above wines would be entitled to be sold as Vin de Pays d'Oc, but this title is usually reserved for those suppliers who may wish to source their grapes from a variety of vineyards, and may switch their supplies from one vintage to the next. The following are some of the best wines from the designation Vin de Pays d'Oc.

Vin de Pays D'Oc

Domaine de Baumière, Hardy's, Béziers (see page 156) – the Australian firm of Hardy's have just started production, mainly from bought-in grapes. The four varieties at present are Sauvignon (soft but with light gooseberry flavours), Chardonnay (a little anonymous, would benefit from a touch of wood-ageing), and two reds, from Merlot and Cabernet, which have not yet been unveiled. Very competently made wines, as long as prices can be kept low enough.

Domaine de Capion, Philippe Salasc, Gignac – one of Daumas Gassac's neighbours, who has started to produce a range of cleanly made varietals.

Domaine de Cazal-Vieil, Henri Miquel, Cessenan – attractive light Sauvignon, fresh and aromatic in style, with good length.

Domaine la Condamine l'Évèque, G. Bascou, Nézignan-l'Évèque – attractive light fruity Syrah with spicy ripe fruit flavours.

Fortant de France, Sète (see page 149) – a range of varietals in distinctive bottles specially designed for the company, with a bunch of grapes embossed on the front. There are three price and quality levels, the top wines coming in smart frosted bottles. Their Chardonnay, which is aged in *barrique*, is attractively smoky and toasty. One of the nicest, and most unusual, is a blush rosé from Cabernet, called Cabernet Gris. Many supermarket own-label varietal wines come from this company.

Gibalaux, SCA du Château Gibalaux, Laure-Minervois – produces an attractive Chardonnay, with a hint of spicy toasty oak flavour.

Le Jeu du Mail, H. Horat & E. Wirz, La Grange de Quatre Sous, Assignan – an interesting new domaine, making unusual wines. The Jeu de Mail is from 60 per cent Marsanne and 40 per cent Viognier, aged (heavily) in new oak. A very good effort, but needs to be lighter on the oak.

Domaine de Raissac, Jean-Luc Viennet, Béziers – a large domaine producing good value reds from Cabernet, Merlot, and an excellent blend of the two.

Vins de Table

There are also a number of wines which have not applied for Vin de Pays status, and are content to be sold as Vin de Table. Apart from the large lake of anonymous and bland wine in this category, there are some quirky, and often very individual wines to be found:

Bouïs Moelleux, Pierre Clément, Guissan – grapey medium sweet white from a blend of various grape varieties. Attractive, light and fruity, a good aperitif wine.

Paul Louis Eugène, Paul Durand, Siran – well-made red and white wines, hand-picked, with small yields. The red, from Carignan and Grenache, is peppery and ripe. The white is the better of the two, lightly oaky, ripe, dry, and with plenty of character.

Worth seeking out.

Vin Favium, Favier-Bel, Frontignan – soft dry white predominantly from Muscat, with slight toffee flavours.

Domaine de la Rectorie, Banyuls-sur-Mer – as well as producing Banyuls, Domaine de la Rectorie produce a red table wine under the label Cuvée Marcellin Reig, which is soft, ripe and spicy. They also produce a *vin naturellement doux*, a wine in the style produced in the last century, from very late-picked, partially dried grapes, without added alcohol. This is unusual and very fine, reminiscent of *vin de paille* or *vin santo*, and makes an excellent aperitif wine.

Vaquer, Fernand Vaquer, Tresserre – a quirky wine from old vines, produced in both red and white, and kept for several years in cask before release. May be France's most expensive Vin de Table. The white is from Maccabéo, and the current vintage is 1978. The red is from Carignan, and is of around the same date. The wines are not cheap, but are very individual and characterful in style, and well known to the local connoisseurs.

7

Faces of Languedoc-Roussillon

A large part of the wine-maker's life is public relations. It is no use making the most wonderful wine in the world if the customers are not there to buy it, or do not know of its existence. Whether the customer is a wine merchant, a supermarket group, a restaurant, or is a local resident or a tourist looking for a few bottles to take back home, he will want to talk to the wine-maker and taste the wines for himself. He will want to see where and how the wines are made, and is more likely to develop a loyalty to the estate if he is well looked after. The wine-maker may have vines to prune, wines to rack or to bottle, orders to dispatch, and a family demanding his attention, but somebody still has to care for the customer, and an important part of the wine-maker's success will depend on this care.

Although some vineyards in Languedoc-Roussillon are in the happy position of being able to sell all their produce without any problem, and a few may even be in the position of rationing their wines to an eager public, the majority need all the customers they can get. The French are accustomed to buying their wine direct, either by mail order or by visiting the vineyard. The problem is merely one of choice. Customers choosing on price are sometimes incredulous when they accidentally stumble on one of the newer young wine-makers who have decided to charge two or three times the price of others in their village. They can become almost abusive, and simply cannot imagine how the grower can justify such blatant robbery. Even if a grower intends to sell his wine for a mere 2 or 3 francs more than that of his neighbours, he may risk losing his customers.

It is a very hard decision to make, and it is the same all the way down the line, from the very cheapest to the very dearest wines of the region. At the bottom end, the grower will take his grapes to a co-operative, or sell them to a *négociant*. The grapes are an annual crop, just like any other, and as such have a market price. The grower's expenses will include the cost of the vines, the land, any chemicals needed for treating the vines during the year, and the costs of labour to prune, care for, and harvest his crop. The price paid will depend on the status of the land (appellation or not), and on the variety grown. It may or may not reflect the quality of the grapes grown.

A table wine producer will be paid per degree alcohol – the largest and ripest crop will give the best financial return, as the grapes will be judged purely on the potential amount of alcohol they can yield. The wine lake is filled to the brim with wines made from grapes grown for quantity and for high sugar content, without thought for flavour, and the EC is offering high monetary incentives to growers to grub up these vines and turn to other crops. Unfortunately, the average French peasant continues to do what he knows best, and as long as high subsidies are paid to him for grapes whose wines are often unsaleable, he will continue happily to grow such grapes.

At the top end of the scale, a grower who takes pains to produce the best possible wine, with small yields, carefully tended vines, and meticulous wine-making, cannot match the price of those with larger crops, and must somehow find customers who will pay the extra costs of quality. This applies as much to a *négociant* selling the basic appellations, to a company making generics, as it does to a small private producer, all of whom must justify that price difference if they are to stay in business.

Here are some examples of people in different walks of life in the wine-maker's world, all with a common aim: to provide the highest quality for today's competitive and often cut-throat market.

The Entrepreneur and Fanatic

Mas de Daumas Gassac, Aniane, 34150 Gignac

'The Lafite of the Languedoc' is how this estate was hailed by the gourmet magazine *Gault Millau* in 1981, after its wine had swept the board at a tasting of the best red wines of France.

The press have continued to eulogize these wines ever since. For journalists looking for an interesting, new and unusual wine property to write about, Mas de Daumas Gassac is a gift from the gods. Not only are the wines superb, but they sell for around ten times the average price of their humble appellation: Vin de Pays de l'Hérault. Aimé Guibert is also a gifted showman, as well as an outstanding wine-maker, and tells the story of the domaine with undiminished enthusiasm and passion to all his visitors, as if each telling were the first. Mas de Daumas Gassac has been added to the list of trendy up-and-coming top-quality estates that must be visited by wine enthusiasts throughout the world, alongside growers such as Eloi Durrbach at Domaine de Trévallon in Les Baux de Provence, Didier Dagueneau in Pouilly-sur-Loire and Alain Brumont of Château Montus in Madiran.

The estate was founded by Aimé and Véronique Guibert de la Vaissière, who bought the property in the early 1970s as a home for themselves and their children, without any thought of wine-making at the time. Situated about half-way between Millau, where Aimé ran a fine leather goods business, and Montpellier, where Véronique taught at the University, it was in an ideal position for commuting. The property included a very small amount of vineyard land, about 5 hectares planted with Aramon, vines of around 120 years of age, but at this stage the Guiberts' idea was to lease the land out for maize production.

The situation changed when the celebrated Professor Enjalbert, an expert on archaeology and geology, visited the estate to view some interesting archaeological relics nearby. Seeing a deep cut in the hillside, where a pathway had been cut through the slope, he was fascinated by the soil structure revealed, which was of a very unusual nature. The valley of Gassac has slopes of 'glacial dust', a mixture of finely ground particles of rock and small angular stones, up to a depth of several metres. Such soil offers a combination of good drainage, very low organic content, and good moisture retention, and Enjalbert recognized that the site, with its similarities to soils of other fine wine regions, had the potential to produce very fine-quality wines.

The soil of the region is unique, 'a miracle' according to Aimé, and has no bearing on the base rock of the valley, or on the soils in the surrounding region. Although very low in organic matter, it has a high iron, copper and boron content. The small stones which form up to 70 per cent of the composition help in moisture retention, and even in drought years the vines always find sufficient moisture for their carefully limited yield. Enjalbert's theory is that the soil may have arrived by tornado, or in some other wind-borne manner. In most regions the final glacial deposits have been washed into rivers, and often out to sea, but outcrops of a similar nature are found in parts of the Médoc and in Burgundy. On his return to Bordeaux, at the request of the Guiberts, Enjalbert sent them a letter twenty-two pages in length, explaining in great depth his theories for the foundation of a great vineyard on the estate, and the reasons for his enthusiasm for their unique soil.

This was in 1972, and the Guiberts started to plan their future as producers of fine wine, undeterred by a complete lack of knowledge or experience in wine-making. Letter in hand, they paid a visit to their friendly bank manager, outlining a plan that would take many years to show financial returns and would necessitate the expenditure of vast sums of money before any returns could even be anticipated.

Vine material was chosen from old-fashioned un-cloned original French vine varieties, to give low yields and 'authenticity'. Nowadays government regulations forbid new vineyards to be planted from any vines that have not been given an official bill of health, and commercial vine propagation must be from specially selected and virus-free vinestocks. Aimé's selection, however, was for quality and flavour, and from vinestocks which would have been officially considered far too low-yielding to be commercially viable. Aimé compares the new cloned vines to a similar technological advance in other plants: 'Look at the apples you can buy today, or the tomatoes – the shapes and sizes are regular and even, the crops are bigger, there is less disease in the plants, but you don't find the flavour that you found years ago, when the fruits may have been smaller and uglier, but tasted of something.'

The choice of vine varieties is interesting and eclectic; alongside the ubiquitous Chardonnay and Cabernet Sauvignon (but in this case very thoughtfully chosen old unmodernized stocks), there is Petit Manseng, a variety not generally found outside the Jurançon, and which was 'borrowed' from 100-year-old vines at Domaine de Rolland.

The Petit Manseng produces only up to 15 or 20 hectolitres per hectare, but gives a very special character to the white wine. In white grapes also, Aimé and Véronique have planted the Viognier of the northern Rhône (vine cuttings from Vernay in Condrieu) alongside small quantities of Marsanne, which they acquired from Clape's vineyards in Cornas.

The white vines were planted only when the Guiberts discovered that part of the land they were planning to plant was not based on the miracle glacial powders, but on limestone. They did not want to alter the character of their red wine by changing the nature of the soil for the red vines, so chose to plant different varieties to make a white wine, the first vintage of which was in 1986.

The vineyards are planted with 80 per cent Cabernet Sauvignon and about 3 per cent each of Merlot, Malbec, Cabernet Franc, Tannat, Syrah and Pinot Noir for the red and rosé wines, and Chardonnay, Viognier, Petit Manseng, Marsanne and Muscat for the whites. The choice was governed by the Guiberts' personal preferences, and by a careful study of quality wine production in other regions of France.

The ripening cycle at Daumas Gassac is generally around three weeks later than in the nearby Gignac Valley, due to the higher elevation and the exposure to cool breezes from the north. The estate is about 200 metres above sea level at its highest point, and so is cool at night, helping the grapes to retain natural acidity. The vineyard of Daumas Gassac is actually around 6°C cooler than the house, which is sheltered in the valley. Only a third of the property is planted in vines, around 25 hectares, as the Guiberts strongly believe that the nature of the region should be preserved and that the surrounding *garrigue* imparts its aromas of thyme, rosemary, wild dog-rose, laburnum and countless other herbs and flowers to the grapes and the wine.

The grapes are picked in 20-kilo picking crates, to avoid undue pressure before they reach the winery. After hand selection of the bunches, the red grapes are pumped by gravity, de-stemmed, and very gently crushed by rubber rollers, taking care not to release the harsh tannins in the pips.

The cellar is built into a Gallo-Roman water mill, and the underground stream of water keeps the floor at a permanent temperature of 12°. The cool temperature helps to prolong the vinification, the top of the *cuve* reaching up to 25° or 30°, automatically percolating through the wine at the bottom of the *cuve*, which has been cooled by the floor temperature. It takes about ten days for the fermentation to be completed. The wines are then put into *barriques*, and the Guiberts have now perfected a system of 'ten ages of wood', with 10 per cent of the casks renewed each year. Each year is then considered separately, and the frequency of racking and length of time the *barriques* are stored bung up varies according to the needs of the wine.

The *barriques* are made from Aliers oak; at first the estate used some second-year barrels from Châteaux Margaux and Palmer, although barrels are now purchased new. The wines spend fifteen to eighteen months in oak, and then, three months before bottling, the different barrels are blended and left to marry in stainless steel. Fining is with white of egg, just before bottling. The wines have the characteristic that they start to mature quite quickly for around two years, then stay at the same level for some time.

White grapes also are vinified in a traditional manner, *débourbage* followed by a maceration on the skins, extracting additional flavouring components from the grape skin. Whites are fermented at between 18° and 20°, which is warmer than most other wineries in the region and is more in line with traditional vinification in the northern Rhône. For both red and white wines, the different varieties are fermented together, and the characteristics of each wine vary slightly with the foibles of the vintage, while keeping a marked individual character of the vineyard. In 1989, for example, the Viognier, a capricious variety, did not flower well, and the wine contains a larger percentage of Chardonnay and Petit Manseng, while in 1988 it flowered successfully, and so 1988 has a greater percentage of Viognier. Petit Manseng has good acidity and a very low pH, even when picked at full ripeness at the end of the vintage, and provides a backbone and firmness to the wine.

After fermentation, and a light filtration, the whites then spend about six weeks in wood before bottling. There is no malolactic fermentation, as the temperature drops quickly after the fermentation because of the cool cellar floor.

Emile Peynaud, the celebrated oenologist from Bordeaux, advises the estate, and originally oversaw all the wine-making, although now the Guiberts have gained more experience and confidence, and make most decisions for themselves. As the focus of so much publicity and attention, many wine-makers visit the estate from other regions of France, and Aimé has to face the barrage of their professional questions, which are occasionally spiced with a hint of jealousy, envy or disbelief. For a self-taught wine-maker, he has come a very long way since the vineyard was first conceived.

The red wines sell for at least 70 or 80 francs a bottle at the cellar door. That is for the current vintage, of which they aim to sell two-thirds to three-quarters to their restaurant and retail customers before the wine is even bottled. Older vintages rise to prices of 300 and 400 francs a bottle or even more. Quantities are so limited that they would rather not sell all the wine. Whites, in even shorter supply, start off at well over 100 francs a bottle, while the rosé is a relative bargain at a mere 40 or 50 francs.

1978 was the first commercial vintage, made from young vines, and is just starting to show its keeping qualities. Later vintages, from more mature vines, look to have even greater potential. Notwithstanding the undoubted quality of the wines, Mas de Daumas Gassac would never have come into being, let alone have sprung to fame, without a personality such as Aimé Guibert to devote both finance and tireless energy to the cause. However, Mas de Daumas Gassac is still several hundred years behind Lafite in its wine-making traditions, and it will take until well into the next century to know exactly how great the potential of the miracle soil will be.

The Young Wine-maker, The Perfectionist

Mas Jullien, 34150 Jonquières

Olivier Jullien was born and raised in the hillsides of Languedoc, where his father and grandfather tended vines whose grapes were processed by the local co-operative. After studying oenology and viticulture, Olivier decided that he wanted to produce and bottle his own wine, and in 1985, at the tender age of twenty, with a diploma in wine production under his belt, he obtained the finance to convert the outbuildings of the family domaine into a cellar, equipped with the basic press, fermentation and storage tanks for his future wine. A number of discreet signs appeared at the road junctions in the tiny village of Jonquières, pointing potential customers in the direction of Mas Jullien, and he has constructed a small reception area at the front of the winery where the wines can be tasted and purchased. There are few wineries of this style in the neighbourhood, and it has taken the locals a few years to get accustomed to Olivier's approach. He has had customers wanting their plastic *bidons* filled, and saying, '. . . But you *must* sell some wine in bulk – the co-operative's closed today!'

Vineyards are quite plentiful in this region; the trick is in choosing only the best sites. Olivier found some ideal parcels of vineyard land to purchase, as well as farming some of the land that already belonged to his family. His 12 hectares of vines are on a number of small sites, mostly around the commune of Jonquières, with some in nearby Cabrières. They are planted with the traditional Grenache, Cinsault, Carignan, Syrah and Mourvèdre. Most of the land was already planted with vines when Olivier took over, and some of the Carignan and Cinsault vines are over forty years old. Because of the range of sites, with their variations in soil, microclimate and variety, Olivier vinifies each site's wine separately, blending the final *cuves* only after a year's maturation in tank. As he becomes more familiar with his 'ingredients' he feels he will have a better instinct for their potential, and will be able to blend sooner.

The red wines are very traditionally produced; some grapes are de-stemmed before crushing where Olivier feels that the stems would give too much bitterness to the wine. The length of *cuvaison* will also depend on the variety, the grapes' ripeness, and on whether they have been de-stemmed. Olivier has added a few oak casks to his cellar over the first few years, but does not believe a wine should taste of oak, keeping most of his wines in stainless steel all their lives to retain their true fruit flavours. His two red *cuvées*, Les Cailloutis and Les Depierre, are bottled after around eighteen months. Les Cailloutis, named after the stony calcareous soils of some two-thirds of his vines, is intended for several years' ageing, and in an ideal world Olivier would rather not sell the wine until it has had time to mature. Les Depierre, a family name, is the lighter of his reds, intended for younger drinking, although this also benefits from a year or two in bottle. The style of these wines changes according to the vintage; in some years Cailloutis has been based on Carignan, others on Syrah.

The problem is that many of Olivier's clients are restaurants, and want to put his wines straight on to their wine lists. He is understandably reluctant to sell them wines which will disappoint their customers if drunk too young, and will even turn away their custom if he does not have stocks of wine which he considers suitable for their purpose. The Depierre, therefore, is more likely to be found on restaurant lists, and Olivier manages to hang on to his Cailloutis for up to a year longer in an effort to prevent his clients from committing the unforgivable sin of drinking his wine before its time has come.

Olivier has also inherited and planted some white varieties: Viognier, Chenin Blanc, Grenache Blanc and Cinsault Blanc. Throughout Languedoc-Roussillon the interest in white wines is increasing, and Olivier says ruefully that 90 per cent of the customer interest is in only 10 per cent of his production, his white wines. Although his production is so limited, Olivier produces two *cuvées* of white, because sometimes the balance of the different varieties would not make a harmonious blend. This practice started in 1989, when his Grenache Blanc was not quite up to scratch as far as he was concerned, and was excluded from his top blend, the Sélection. With this 'inferior' wine, he decided to experiment with oak-ageing, and gave the white Grenache a short ageing in new *barriques* before bottling, thus reversing the practice of most wine-makers, who will spare the expense of new oak only on their top wines.

In 1990, his second *cuvée* of white, labelled Les Cépages Oubliées, was from a blend of Terret-Bourret, Carignan Blanc and Grenache Blanc, fermented in new oak. The Carignan Blanc was from a parcel of eighty-year-old vines belonging to his grandfather, which he had not originally intended to use. 'The wine could have been much more intense if he had not had such a large yield,' Olivier said sadly. Why? How large was the yield? 'Oh, almost 50 hectolitres per hectare!' This in a region where many producers are disappointed with a yield as low as 80. He also produced a small amount of rosé wine from Carignan with oak-ageing. In each case the oak is intended to add a little extra to the wine's flavour, rather than to give too much flavour of its own.

Olivier feels that his wines should express the character of their *terroir*, and believes passionately in the quality of the traditional and long-established varieties originally responsible for the quality reputation of his region. Why change to the more fashionable varieties or to the fashionable oak-aged flavours of today's transient market when he can produce wines that express the potential quality of the much-maligned Carignan and Cinsault?

Olivier's wine is starting to gain recognition, a fact about which he is naturally thrilled; the only drawback is that he had hoped to spend his life making wine, and is now finding that he has to spend more and more time on administration.

He and his young wife Carole are shy, charming and immensely earnest and enthusiastic ambassadors for the Coteaux du Languedoc.

New World Technology – The Businessman of the Future

Robert Skalli, Fortant de France, Skalli, route de Montpellier, 44204 Sète

When you buy a bottle of varietally labelled Languedoc wine from any of the supermarket chains in the UK, the chances are very high that it will have been produced by Skalli, the Mondavi of the south of France.

The Skalli family enterprise, with a turnover in excess of £300 million per annum, is based on the major agricultural products of Languedoc-Roussillon: rice, cereals and wine. All are approached from the modern, marketing point of view, with emphasis equally on packaging, on product image, and on the indispensable value-for-money aspect. Robert Skalli, the president of the wine side of the business, is no poet or romantic with his head in the clouds, but a dynamic, energetic businessman with a flair for presentation, and his finger on the pulse of modern market forces.

The Skalli enterprise have over 600 hectares of vineyards in the Napa Valley and some 550 hectares in Corsica, in addition to their Languedoc-Roussillon wine-making venture. The concept is to provide creative varietal wines at cheaper prices, with a team of tasters including Californian, Australian, British and French wine experts to help choose the blends. While they do not produce any great wines, the aim is to produce sound wines at the right price. This is blending at its finest, with each constituent of the blend carefully costed, and a well-crafted final product combining high-tech wine expertise with careful monitoring of consumer appeal. Over 105,000 cases a year are exported to the USA, Fortant's largest export market, with the UK and Japan as other main overseas buyers.

Robert Skalli firmly believes that the future of the wine market, especially in the lower-priced, everyday band, depends upon varietals rather than on geographic origin, the consumer having more confidence in the branding of 'Chardonnay' and 'Cabernet' than of 'Corbières' or 'Minervois'. Wines are all produced under the designation Vin de Pays d'Oc, the lowest common denomination for Languedoc-Roussillon, allowing wines to be blended from anywhere throughout the region, according to availability. The wines are found under the firm's name, Fortant de France, as well as under a multitude of other brand names to suit their customers, who generally prefer to have their own name on the label.

The firm started negotiating long-term contracts with growers in Languedoc-Roussillon in 1982, offering three-, six- or nine-year contracts to growers who would agree to grow and supply the varietals needed. Some fifty growers are under contract at present, and the trend is growing, with more eager to join. Each grower contracts to plant some or all of his vineyard with one or more of the varieties chosen from Skalli's shopping list. Points are awarded on the contract for variety, yield, and vinification equipment. Growers opting for white wine production, for example, would be expected to install cold fermentation equipment, with temperature-controlled vats. The contract guarantees to buy the wine produced, at good market rates, as long as the quality criteria are maintained, and the grower can negotiate any bank loans required for modernization of his vineyard on the strength of the contract. The vines and the land remain the property of the grower, who can opt out and produce and sell his own wine at the end of the contract term if he so wishes.

Growers receive advice from viticultural experts, and from oenologists who visit each domaine and follow the vinification process. Some of the wine is vinified in the giant modern 'factory' in Sète, the rest is brought to Sète in bulk after vinification at the domaine. There are three units, one for treatment and vinification of the wines, one entirely devoted to barrel-ageing, and one for bottling the wines. As an indication of the firm's priorities, there are only about twenty employees at work in the factory, compared to some thirty-five to forty employed in marketing, and around twelve trained oenologists.

The barrel-ageing unit is particularly reminiscent of the New World, housing up to 2,000 new oak *barriques*, some from American oak, with a selection of all the French oak styles available. The oak is intended to impart a maximum flavour, and casks are changed every two to three years. Although much of the barrel fermentation used to take place in the individual growers' cellars in early years, it is now being transferred to headquarters, where the oenologists can keep better control of the wines.

The bottling unit combines a hint of space age with modern good taste. Following the age-old theory that the customer, however humble, likes to see where and how the wine is made, Skalli have built a customer reception centre around the bottling plant, which has received some 20,000 visitors a year during the two years since it opened. Visitors follow cool marble-lined corridors around the building, stopping at various vantage points where a hand-held walkie-talkie explains the wine in the language of your choice. The customers see a short film explaining the varieties and the wines produced, and then watch through glass picture windows as the bottling line sweeps the bottles past their gaze along the fully automated line. Paintings and works of art by modern artists line the route, until the customer reaches the final point of the tour, a tasting room, with a souvenir shop selling not just the wines, but also T-shirts and other vinous items to remember their trip and the name of Fortant. Future plans include a concept of wafting perfumes into the corridor when the varieties are being explained: blackcurrant for the Cabernet and gooseberry for the Sauvignon, to help with customer recognition of the wines produced.

Robert Skalli is aware of the customer in a way that few large or small wine-makers will ever manage. As he strides energetically through the corridors, nothing seems to escape his notice. Flexibility of approach and management abilities combine with flair and artistic skill to produce state-of-the-art wines at sensible prices.

Cheap, but Not the Cheapest – The Businessman of the Present Day

Maison Jeanjean, St-Félix-de-Lodez, 34150 Gignac

Robert Skalli looks to the future from where Maison Jeanjean have shown the way – or so Bernard Jeanjean would like to believe. The Jeanjean family have been *négociants* since the 1870s, originally selling wines *en vrac*, in bulk, from a horse and cart, and progressing to become one of the region's largest and most important *négociant* houses, selling around 800 million hectolitres a year, 80 per cent of this from Languedoc-Roussillon. The main expansion has been over the last twenty years, when Bernard and Hugues took over the firm's management from their father. They have worked long and hard to improve the quality image of their region, concentrating on selling wines of the different appellations within Languedoc-Roussillon, and trying in each case to supply the best of each appellation at a reasonable price.

Their wines are far from the cheapest *négociant* wines, and Bernard Jeanjean finds it frustrating that so often the region's wines are bought and sold on price alone. 'If the consumer is faced with two bottles of Corbières on the supermarket shelf, one at 8 francs and one at 12 francs, how is he supposed to choose? The only difference between the two is the *négociant*'s name, which the consumer probably does not know.' He finds that his supermarket clients show the greatest resistance to wines that will retail above 18 francs, and the largest market is in the cheapest wines. Indeed, Jeanjean's greatest seller is table wine in plastic bottles, most of which is sold within France. Some 450,000 hectolitres per year are sold in plastic by Maison Jeanjean, the equivalent of 30 million 1.5-litre bottles.

This is probably the most tricky end of the market; there has to be sufficient margin to make a profit for the wine-grower, the *négociant* and the supermarket company, and still to sell the wine at a price that will attract the customer, probably a maximum of 7 or 8 francs for 1.5 litres. At this price, wines are purchased for neutrality and lack of faults rather than for intrinsic quality or flavour, and the job is more that of the chemist and the accountant than that of the wine-lover.

At the higher-quality level wines are purchased by appellation, and also by individual domaine or château. The problem is in finding sufficient supplies at an interesting price, and Maison Jeanjean purchases their wines from a wide range of sources including co-operatives and private domaines. Often the private domaines will be happy to sell off their less good wines, keeping the best for their own use, but Jeanjean also list a number of domaine-bottled wines for which they have exclusivity, including Dame Adelaide in Corbières, Domaine St-Martin in Fitou, and Château Pierreru in St-Chinian. In each case, what they are seeking is the best quality available within their price range.

The laboratory at Maison Jeanjean processes some ninety samples a day, selecting wines to buy, and testing the wines both before and after buying and after bottling. Wines are purchased after fermentation, and are either shipped at that time, or perhaps after some ageing at the grower's cellars. At every stage the wines need to be tasted and analysed. Many of their supermarket customers are becoming highly conscious of the technical side of wine-buying, and it is quite common for a prospective client to send their chemist to visit the factory before they even think of sending their wine-buyer. In this respect, Jeanjean find that the British and Danish customers are the most finicky.

Bernard Jeanjean sees his role in promoting the region's wines as that of improving and maintaining the image of Languedoc-Roussillon as an entity. He complains that there are too many sub-regional promotional bodies, and too much emphasis on splitting the region into ever-decreasing sub-appellations, without sufficient emphasis on increasing the minimum quality levels for the appellations already in existence. His sales of appellation wines are decreasing in favour of wines with the Vin de Pays designation, which sell for almost the same price and are often the better wines. With the increased permitted yield over appellation wines, Vins de Pays provide a better return for the wine-maker. He sees this as a worrying trend for the future of the appellation system of the region as a whole.

'It's a funny thing,' mused Bernard Jeanjean. 'Ecologically, the plastic bottle makes far more sense than the traditional glass bottle. It cuts the weight by half as well as taking much less space in the delivery lorry, therefore reducing transport costs. It does not need recycling, which in itself involves higher energy and transport costs, and it does not waste cork.'

Maison Jeanjean does not have gleaming new buildings and state-of-the-art offices. The appearance is homely and practical, that of a firm keeping its overheads down to a minimum. Its great strength is that of Bernard and Hugues Jeanjean, whose personality and experience in matching the customers to the wines of their region that will best suit their purpose has done much to promote Languedoc-Roussillon to the everyday drinking public both in France and abroad.

Château Coujan, 34490 Murviel

François Guy and his sister Solange Peyre are the fifth generation of wine-makers to live and work at Château Coujan since their ancestors bought the domaine in 1852. This is not one of the self-consciously beautiful properties, but is a very attractive working château, with rows of enormous wooden vats built into large ivy-covered *chais*, and with its ancient stone walls smothered with Virginia creeper, a beautiful sight in the autumn. Peacocks and dogs wander past the front of the domaine, and the effect is that of a well-loved family home. A stone table in front of the house is stacked with chunks of fossilized rock for the customers to take as a souvenir, a reminder that the soil here is rich in fossil deposits. There are still some vestiges of an eleventh-century chapel on the site, and most of the buildings are several centuries old.

François Guy is a showman who takes immense pleasure in discussing his wines with any potential customer, whether large or small. There is no sense of urgency, and no sales pressure. Customers are guided through the range of wines available, to the accompaniment of a gentle and amusing dialogue from Monsieur Guy. All tastes are catered for, from a crisp dry white Vin de Pays from the Sauvignon grape to big, firm, classic full-flavoured red St-Chinian.

Château Coujan try to hold stocks of older vintages for both restaurant and private customers, and there are stocks of wines back to the 1976 Vin de Pays, still showing very good fruit flavours.

The best St-Chinian in the best vintages is sold under the label Cuvée Gabrielle de Spinola, in memory of a former landowner, the Marquise de Spinola, who used to have the first 500 litres of the best wine of Château Coujan as part of the rent in the late 1700s. The St-Chinian is from a blend of Mourvèdre, Cinsault, Grenache and Syrah. François Guy is not a fan of Carignan, finding it too rustic, and preferring Mourvèdre, which he has planted increasingly since 1982. His 1985 Cuvée Spinola is rich, gamey and spicy, a marvellous wine.

When the Vin de Pays legislation permitted other varieties to be planted in the region, he planted Cabernet Sauvignon, Merlot and Sauvignon Blanc, starting in 1967. His Merlot Cabernet blend has been produced since 1970, although it has only been vintage-dated since 1976. In most vintages the wine is made from 75 per cent Merlot and 25 per cent Cabernet, aged for about a year in wood, although in concentrated vintages such as 1985 the wine may spend up to three years in wood before bottling. It is softer in style than the St-Chinian, with elegant gentle mellow fruit flavours. As a Vin de Pays, it is not entitled to the Château name on the label, and is sold simply as Guy & Peyre Vin de Pays des Coteaux du Murviel.

White Coteaux du Languedoc is produced from a blend of Rolle and Grenache Blanc, as well as a white Vin de Pays from Sauvignon. Neither owes much to the vaunted modern technology of some of the larger estates, and both are well-made traditional wines with good flavour and individual character.

François Guy epitomizes the old-style wine domaine, selling to large numbers of private customers as well as to a number of restaurants and retailers. Many of his customers have been buying from the domaine for a long time, some Parisian customers assuring us proudly that they had been buying his wines for many years, to put in their cellars alongside their first-growth clarets. 'In the end,' they concurred, 'it is very good quality for the price, and we cannot drink 1947 Mouton every day.'

At 12.30 p.m. one day, as we were taking our leave of Monsieur Guy and his sister was just about to put his lunch on the table, another car-load of visitors arrived at his gate. Without anyone blinking an eyelid, lunch was returned to the oven and François Guy went out cheerfully and courteously to greet the newcomers, leading them off with unabated enthusiasm to the *cave* for another lengthy session of wine-tasting. Customer service is always important, and you can see exactly why his customers always come back.

The Wine-maker Who Does Not Sell Wine

Guy and Marc Benin, Domaine de Ravanès, 34490 Thézan-les-Béziers

'Can we come and visit you briefly next Sunday morning?' we had asked. Sunday morning is not always a popular time as far as wine-makers are concerned, but we had booked a table for lunch at our favourite restaurant in the Languedoc, and Sunday is the only day that they open for lunch. Hence Sunday morning is a popular time for us to visit wine-makers in the vicinity. 'Yes,' was the reply, 'but not *too* briefly – you will need at least two hours to taste my wines.'

On the Sunday morning we dutifully raced to the small town of Thézan-les-Béziers, well on schedule for once. A signpost in the village set us on route for Domaine de Ravanès, but then the signposts seemed to lose interest and we had to work on instinct, which led us to a large, rambling, and seemingly deserted group of buildings, just as the road petered out. At last a clue – a gleaming mechanical harvester stood in the yard. This must be the home of a wine domaine, but was it the right one? Our instincts were right for once, and we had arrived on time, leaving a good two hours for the tasting before we had to drive to the restaurant.

Guy Benin proved to be an energetic, enthusiastic man with an infectious laugh and a passion for talking. It turned out that he and his son had booked a table at the same restaurant as us for lunch, as their wives had gone away on a jaunt for the weekend. At least they would understand the need for punctuality.

His son, Marc Benin, is a doctor of oenology and has introduced several innovations of his own, such as a botrytis Ugni Blanc in 1989. His father has never made white wines – 'As I have gout, I only ever drink red wine, never white,' he claims. He also grows several varieties that he never vinifies himself, as he is not too keen on the type of wine they produce. Why not replant with his preferred varieties? 'Oh, because I planted those vines when I first bought the estate, I don't like to change them.' The grapes are harvested and sold to other producers.

The wine that Guy Benin vinifies on the estate is from Merlot, Cabernet Sauvignon, or a blend of the two, with a touch of Petit Verdot, another grape from Bordeaux. The vines were planted in the mid 60s, and these are the varieties that he admires and that suit his style of wine-making. The wines are vinified and aged in stainless steel tanks. He has experimented with oak *barriques*, but does not feel that his wine needs to have oak for added complexity. As an experiment, some 1980 has been stored in stainless steel, and not bottled. In 1991 this was still tasting remarkably fresh and lively, with mellow ripe fruit flavours and no signs of fading.

Guy Benin's father was a *négociant* and blender of wines from North Africa. He had very little sense of smell, so Guy was called in to assist with tasting the wines from a very early age and developed a highly trained palate while still in his teens. One of his father's tests on wine was to leave a bottle open for a month, tasting at various stages during that time. 'Most wines will have oxidized completely during that length of time, but it is useful to see if the wine develops any other problems; it is a good test of the health of the wine.'

Domaine de Ravanès is a large domaine, and the wines are shipped to several countries, including the UK, Ireland, America, Canada, and a number of European countries. Guy Benin, however, does not see himself as a seller of wine. 'I enjoy making wine,' he says, 'and I enjoy meeting people. I like to get to know the people who are interested in trading in my wine before we do business. You see, I don't sell my wine, I only exchange it for money.' He tells the story of a Swiss wine merchant who visited the domaine. He asked if his chemist could take some samples, to which Guy readily agreed. However, on entering his cellar, he found the chemist on his knees taking swabs from the floor, the walls, the table, and all around the cellar. 'What are you doing?' he cried. 'I thought you wanted to take samples of my wine, not my floor. What if I had just stepped in a dog mess before entering the cellar? Would that affect the quality of my wine? I keep my premises clean, but I'm selling the wine, not the premises.' The Swiss merchant and his chemist were shown the door.

After we had seen the cellar, Guy and Marc took us to the tasting room, a modern, well-laid-out area resplendent with a huge American flag, in honour of his US clients, and with a display of press clippings from the domaine's numerous mentions in print. A splendid tasting of a decade of the domaine's wines was enlivened by a constant stream of anecdotes from father and son, both of whom have travelled and tasted widely, and both of whom are passionately interested in all aspects of wine. Each wine was analysed and discussed at length before passing to the next vintage. By the time we had finished, we all realized that we were extremely late for lunch. Luckily Guy knew a 'short cut', and our car sped along behind his – not too close behind, as he was still holding an earnest conversation with Marc, swerving in and out of the oncoming traffic in true French style as he waved his arms in the air to emphasize the point under discussion.

Guy and Marc Benin love their life as *vignerons*. They are not courting the journalists or the wine merchants. They are looking for conviviality and an interest in wine from their visitors – then they are willing to exchange some of their wine against cash.

The New World Invasion

Bill Hardy, Domaine des Baumes, Béziers

After the Penfold's/Lindeman's conglomerate, and the Yalumba Winery, Hardy's is probably the third largest Australian wine producer. Bill Hardy, one of Hardy's directors and a dedicated francophile, explained that they sense that the Australian market is declining at present, and the company therefore decided a few years ago to look at new potential markets. Feeling that the French had not really exploited the possible market for varietal wines, they decided that this could be an opening for Hardy's – a combination of Australian technology, economies of scale, and a competitive price would produce New World style varietals for the overseas market.

The company had scrutinized available French vineyard sites over several years, and had come up with the Domaine des Baumes, a large but run-down property on the outskirts of Béziers. The domaine has 61 hectares of land, but only 5 under vine at present. The cellars, which had not been in use for a few years, were full of mouldy and dilapidated wooden vats and had to be completely rebuilt, but at least they could be rebuilt entirely to Hardy's specifications. They have installed a plant room, with all the motors for refrigeration, air compressors and other machinery. As Bill Hardy says, it keeps all the noisy smelly bits in one place, well away from the cellar.

The grand plan was always to buy in the majority of fruit, rather than to grow the grapes themselves, and brokers throughout Languedoc-Roussillon provided grapes from twenty growers for the first vintage in 1990. The majority of these grapes were mechanically harvested, allowing the varieties to be picked and transported at night, when the temperatures are at their coolest. The furthest vineyards for the first crop were in Limoux, where the cooler vineyard region produces Chardonnay and Cabernet Sauvignon grapes with excellent acidity balance, something which is often missing in the warmer regions. Grapes from Limoux can take six hours to arrive at the winery, but as these grapes are hand-picked, the skins are intact, and with an addition of sulphur dioxide the grapes travel without any undue damage.

One of the major differences in Hardy's technology is that the grapes are cooled during crushing, the speed of the crush determining the degree of refrigeration. The white juice is chilled down to around 5°C to clear the must before fermentation, and the red is cooled to about 15°C. Banks of sophisticated machinery can regulate the temperature as required, and few staff are needed in the winery, as most tasks can be performed on the flick of a button.

Bill Hardy has an Australian wine-maker, Peter Dawson, who visits the estate at vintage time from Western Australia. He has also employed a cellar-master from Montpellier, but the rest of his staff consists of two builders with an interest in wine-making. With their qualifications they are handy if any improvements or repairs to the cellars are needed, and they do not have any preconceived ideas as to how wine should be made. Bill would rather teach them wine technology, Australian-style, from scratch.

Bill admits to a few hiccups in these early days – some of the expensive machinery is under-utilized. For example, an expensive rotary vacuum filter which can extract the very last drop of clean juice from the lees is an essential part of Hardy's Australian wine-making technique. In France, however, where each grower has to submit a certain quantity of *marc*, lees or if necessary wine for distillation into alcohol as a state tax, it is pointless cleaning the last drop of juice. Also, the transport of grapes in southern France is somewhat different from in Australia. A vineyard may be just down the road as the crow flies, but narrow roads and bridges with weight restrictions often necessitate lengthy and unforeseen deviations. At one vineyard, the lorry transporting the grapes could not fit through the stone gateway at the entrance, and the crates of grapes had to be driven in batches by forklift truck down two kilometres of bumpy driveway to load the lorry outside the gate.

The bad frosts in France in 1991 also set back Bill's plans for the year. Chardonnay and Sauvignon Blanc were both severely affected by the frosts, and in short supply. Growers were unwilling even to quote a price for these grapes until vintage time, when grapes went to the highest bidder. In 1990 Bill was paying about 5.50 francs a kilo for Chardonnay grapes, double the price of other varieties. In 1991 the price was between 6 and 7 francs, a hefty increase for a winery that is trying to keep its costs low. The quantities vinified were also lower than anticipated, because there were fewer grapes available.

Local growers have a very mixed attitude to the company, and to the numerous other overseas companies who have moved in on Languedoc-Roussillon vineyards. While grateful for the high prices achieved for many of the vineyards they have sold, and for the employment created, there are still many who mutter about the bread taken from the mouths of the locals, and who strongly resent the invasion by foreigners. Bill and his wife are the type of foreigners it is hard to resent for long; down to earth, with a genuine interest in the region, and no wish to create enemies.

Bill Hardy and his company have invested very heavily in this venture, and Domaine des Baumes is in many ways a rather unlikely choice, as it is an old building with many inconveniences. The costs of technology may well take longer to recuperate than Hardy's at first supposed, but in any case both the French and the Australians will learn a thing or two along the way.

The Pension Fund

Mas de la Garrigue, 66240 St-Estève

The annual *Guide Hachette des Vins de France* is one of our indispensable companions when searching for wines for our shop, and many superb discoveries have resulted from following their recommendations. So when searching for old Rivesaltes wines, what more natural than to look up their comments for the region? Mas de la Garrigue is in St-Estève, not far from Perpignan, and is not easy for the uninitiated to find. Eventually, with a little guidance, we located the unremarkable large square private house, set back a little way in the suburban street, with no external signs that we had located an outstanding wine-producer. An elderly lady appeared at the upstairs window to inquire who we were, and what we wanted, while an elderly man who had been dawdling in the sunshine down the road appeared with mild curiosity to see that we were not up to any mischief.

When told that we wished to buy some wine, Madame descended and welcomed us into the house, surprised but pleased that we were interested in the Vieux Rivesaltes. The loafer also came over to join us, and to add his warm recommendation of the wines. It was a sad story: the daughter who had been helping to run the domaine had been tragically killed in a car accident some years previously, and the old couple had lost heart and completely lost their enthusiasm to continue without her. Her father had had a stroke, and was now partially incapacitated, leaving mother to try to continue the business more or less single-handed.

Mas de la Garrigue belongs to the Vila family. One brother lives in the Mas, further away from Perpignan among the vineyards, while the other lives with his wife in the house at St-Estève. Behind the modest façade in St-Estève a series of large glass-lined concrete vats contain vast quantities of Vieux Rivesaltes, going back to the 1959 vintage and including only a few carefully chosen vintages. Marcel Vila has unerringly selected only the vintages which have sufficient quality to age and to improve for many years, and which he considers a worthy investment.

The wines are bottled as and when required, and have wonderful ripe cherry and prune flavours, with subtle hints of mocha chocolate, raisins and caramel toffee. Apart from the Rivesaltes, entirely from Grenache Noir, the only other wines produced are a small amount of Muscat de Rivesaltes, more or less discontinued now as they do not have the fashionable cold fermentation equipment, and their wine is unfashionably golden, soft and fruity in flavour. There is also occasionally a table wine from Grenache Noir, redolent with the same ripe prune and plum flavours as the Rivesaltes. Wines are made traditionally, with little interference from man, and with nature left to take its course as much as possible.

To taste the wines in vat, Madame led the way up a precarious stairway to the roof of the vats and dipped in a battered saucepan to scoop up some of the delicious nectar. She chattered volubly and enthusiastically in broad lilting Catalan French while we, and even the fluent French speakers, strained to follow the conversation. A very generous and kindly hostess, she sent out for a packet of the special local biscuits that go so well with the wine, and which we had never tried. Not only did we sample the wine with a variety of cakes and biscuits at the house, but some more packets had been put on one side for us to take home. It is hard to leave the Vilas without being given some little gift – home-made apricot jam, a big bag of fresh apricots, or some special wine.

We have even tried to persuade Madame and her husband that their prices are far too cheap for the old vintages, but their accountant has told them that they must sell more wine, and they are reluctant to increase the price. Understandably, they do not want to put up large advertising hoardings to entice the tourists to buy – it would take a great deal of time and effort, and require someone to be on hand every day to deal with tasting and sales. You can, however, be assured of a very warm and enthusiastic welcome once you reach the domaine, as well as a chance to buy some of the most undervalued wine of Languedoc-Roussillon.

The Restaurateur

Restaurant Le Mimosa, 34150 St-Guiraud

Love of France, and of food and wine, led David and Bridget Pugh to become restaurateurs. David was a musician by trade, and Bridget a ballet dancer, which can still be seen in her graceful stance. They had bought a remote holiday home in the hills of Languedoc, and had fallen so thoroughly in love with the area that they decided to give up the bright lights and move to France full-time. As Bridget was an excellent cook, and David a keen wine buff, they decided to start a restaurant, neither having had any experience whatsoever in the catering trade. This is a familiar story, and there must be many husband and wife restaurant teams that have started optimistically with little more practical experience than a love of cooking and entertaining.

Few, however, can compare with the Pughs in achievement. Having purchased a large *provençal* house with courtyard in the tiny village of St-Guiraud, they converted the main room into a dining room, put together an eclectic list of wines, and proceeded to launch the restaurant. The local villagers hardly expected them to last out the year, and were confidently pessimistic. The French are notoriously particular about the quality of their food, and also have very set ideas about wines. Bridget has introduced them to such gastronomic delights as pavlova and crumble, while David has persuaded them to try some of the excellent local wines rather than sticking rigidly to Bordeaux.

The fame of Le Mimosa has spread rapidly, and customers travel from far and wide. They have to – there is no hotel or other accommodation in St-Guiraud, and the nearest towns to stay in are Clermont l'Hérault or Gignac, both some ten kilometres away. Le Mimosa has been helped by the fact that it is close to Mas de Daumas Gassac, one of the region's most prestigious wineries. Conversely, Mas de Daumas Gassac is helped by being close to Le Mimosa, an excellent ambassador and showcase for their wines.

David takes a wicked pleasure in filling in the questionaires from restaurant guides: 'Where did you train as a *sommelier*?' – nowhere. 'Where did your wife train as a chef?' – nowhere. 'What style of food do you offer?' – all sorts of styles. It depends on the inspiration of the day, on what is fresh at the local market. The Pughs do not want to be branded as *nouvelle cuisine, provençal cuisine*, or any of the other buzz-words. One restaurant guide has them earmarked as '*nouvelle gastronomique exotique provençale*', which seems as accurate as any description can be. Bridget has persuaded local nursery gardeners to plant more unusual herbs and vegetables, and will also experiment with old-fashioned plants such as wild leeks, generally considered a weed, which grow in the local vineyards. The important factor is that all the ingredients are fresh, and the cooking sensitive and imaginative.

Building up a restaurant wine cellar is a costly and time-consuming business. David started with a small but select range of high-quality wines, and is constantly tempted to increase the number. As the restaurant becomes better known, he is increasingly courted by the local wine-makers, who would all love the prestige of being included on his select wine list. His excellent palate, and his strict selection of only the very best, mean that his pronouncements on a wine are anxiously awaited by growers, and his advice often sought. On Mondays, when the restaurant is closed, he regularly visits growers throughout the region, tasting and discussing the wines and building up an encyclopedic knowledge of the region. While writing this book, I had constant admonishments from David: '. . . You absolutely *must* visit so-and-so . . . You cannot possibly omit this or that winery, they are doing such interesting things . . . Have you tried this property's wines? I think you'll like them.'

One large group of clients included an overseas ambassador and his party, and his chauffeur, who ate at a separate table on the patio outside. Having checked that his bill was being taken care of by the main party, and that he could choose whatever he liked from the menu, David took the chauffeur's order. 'Just water with your meal?' he asked diffidently. 'No, what are the main party drinking? I'll have a glass of that.' When the next course arrived, he inquired, 'What are the main party drinking now?' and duly had a glass. The next course was met with the now familiar query, and this time the chauffeur asked the waiter to leave the rest of the bottle with him. After a number of courses, with their accompanying wines, the chauffeur was still sober but benign, and thanked David and Bridget effusively for a wonderful lunch.

Le Mimosa tends to attract the British and other overseas visitors who have holiday homes in the area, but only those with a reasonable budget. Although cheap by London restaurant standards, a meal for two with wine will cost in the region of 750 francs. The clientele also includes a number of wine-makers, both local and from afar – Auguste Clape from the Rhône is a regular visitor, and other guests have included Monsieur Reynaud from Château Rayas, and Angelo Gaja from Piedmont in Italy.

One of David's many talents is an extraordinary memory. The dessert trolley at Le Mimosa is a delight to behold, with a choice of *gâteaux* and pastries, as well as *compôtes* of fruit and a daily choice of home-produced sorbets and ice-creams. The trolley is wheeled to the table, the various delights described, and customers urged to mix and match to their hearts' delight. The orders might be taken for several tables at the same time, and David never writes anything down. A nod and a smile, and he wheels the trolley away with a flourish, returning shortly with plates of assorted goodies, each unerringly placed in front of the right customer.

Customers, whether tourists or locals, often want advice in choosing their wines, and David loses no opportunity to promote the wines of his beloved Languedoc. Although he will provide customers with excellent Bordeaux or Burgundy wines, by the time he has finished extolling the virtues of Faugères, St-Chinian and Coteaux du Languedoc, most of the clients are happy to follow his advice. 'The problem is,' he says, 'I often end up selling the customer a much less expensive wine than the one they were originally thinking of.' This is true devotion to the region.

8

A Look at the Future

Emile Peynaud remarked that it is only the top 5 per cent of Bordeaux wines which project the image of Bordeaux as a whole. Languedoc-Roussillon has not developed a top 5 per cent yet, although it has a very firmly rooted image based on the bottom 60 per cent of its production. The problem now is to change the public's conception of the region.

Languedoc-Roussillon has been described as a region which almost died, and which is now slowly coming back to life. This is probably a very accurate description. As we have seen, the history shows the usual ebb and flow of any wine region, with periods of prosperity interspersed with periods of over-production. However, whereas in previous centuries natural market forces acted as a constraint to over-production, and only the fittest survived any recession, in this century the state and EC policies have provided subsidies which unnaturally cushion the less efficient producer.

The incentive to produce top-quality wine in a region such as Languedoc-Roussillon, with its low-priced image, is very small. However, economies of scale can lead to very competitively priced wines from large producers such as Salins du Midi and Fortant de France, and the comparatively cheap price of land in the Midi has led to substantial investments from wine companies based both in other parts of France and abroad. The last ten years have seen newcomers such as Peter Sichel from Bordeaux and Hardy's from Australia, attracted by the opportunities to plant large tracts of land and to produce almost New World style varietal wines.

Many of the appellations are very recent, a number dating only from 1985, and in their first decade of life. Many are still modifying their rules over a period of the next ten or twenty years, to allow growers time to re-plant with the revised proportions of permitted varieties. There is a multitude of appellations, many with separate regional committees for promotion, and with little generic promotion of Languedoc-Roussillon as a whole. The introduction of Vin de Pays legislation has further complicated matters, adding a further sixty-seven possible designations for the wines of the region. Although this was not the purpose of the legislation, a grower can now legally   over-produce, selling the regulated amount as appellation wine and the surplus identical wine under the Vin de Pays designation.

While sales of appellation wines are generally slightly down within the region, sales of Vin de Pays are showing a substantial increase. Consumers are becoming increasingly aware of varietals, which are easier to recognize and relate to than generic regions. From Bulgarian Cabernet Sauvignon to Australian Chardonnay, the consumer remembers the grape name more easily than the region or the producer's name. The supermarket and off-licence chains have a large choice of inexpensive wines from these popular varieties, and the customer is unlikely to remember whether the wine is Vin de Pays d'Oc or Vin de Pays de l'Hérault, if indeed he realizes that the wine he is drinking is from southern France.

Only a handful of grape varieties have fashionable kudos: after the ubiquitous Chardonnay and Cabernet Sauvignon come Sauvignon Blanc, Pinot Noir, Merlot and Syrah, with less widely seen varieties such as Viognier, Marsanne and Mourvèdre now starting to become trendy. Many of the traditional varieties of Languedoc-Roussillon have a very negative consumer appeal, often rightly so, and it is good that high-yielding neutral-flavoured varieties such as Aramon and Alicante Bouschet should be reduced or even eliminated. It must be remembered, however, that varieties such as Carignan and Cinsault can, in the right soil and with the right yield, produce very good wines. Far too many people take as gospel that Cabernet Sauvignon is always going to be better than either of these, regardless of site. The historic reputation of regions such as Faugères and St-Chinian, for example, is due to Carignan and Cinsault, and insistence on a percentage of Mourvèdre in the current appellation is in fact changing the character of the wine. Mourvèdre was introduced to these regions only within the last twenty years, and so a new style of wine has been created by law, replacing the traditional style of the last 200 years.

Many wines in Languedoc-Roussillon are made and bought by chemists, whose hygiene specifications are often more vital than intrinsic quality considerations. In any case, today's society is not used to having too much flavour in their foods or their wines, and a cheap wine without obvious character is far easier to sell than one which smells and tastes strongly. I have been asked, 'Is this wine meant to smell?', and a fellow wine merchant has been asked accusingly, 'Why does this wine *taste*?' While prices paid to producers of appellation wines can be as low as 3 francs a litre in bulk, there is little incentive to rock the boat, and the customer will be given what he thinks he wants.

On the positive side, however, things are looking up for Languedoc-Roussillon. Outside investors are bringing money into the region, and giving growers the financial incentive to improve quality. Freedom to choose what to plant and what style of wine to make has attracted growers from the more constrained areas of Bordeaux and Burgundy to invest in the region, all of which adds to its increasing prestige and improves its quality image. Many more young wine-makers are being encouraged to start up, in regions where ten or twenty years ago the majority of growers were nearing retirement age.

Instead of being seen as a financial liability to the French state, Languedoc-Roussillon is gaining a reputation as a good investment risk, and the scramble to find suitable vineyard land is gathering momentum in a manner far more reminiscent of California or Australia than of France.

There will always be a market for a well-made, individual style of wine, and the new generation of young growers have the energy and enthusiasm to take on this challenge. There is a rise in the number of 'boutique' wines appearing on the market, widening the hitherto narrow price bracket achieved for Vins de Pays and minor appellations. Languedoc-Roussillon may be the first wine area of France to abandon its newly gained appellations in favour of the freedom to experiment with new styles and varieties.

What will change over the next ten or twenty years? There is increased interest in white wine production, and modern technology has made it possible to produce clean, attractive fruity wines where once the whites were somewhat dull and flabby. The scramble to plant white varieties, and to re-graft red vines to white, will result in oceans of pleasant, cleanly made but largely undistinguished wines coming on to stream in five to ten years' time. Will some growers not kick themselves eventually for having followed the crowd, when fashions move forward, and maybe full-bodied red wines stage a comeback? We have seen this happen in Australia and California, where superb old vines were obliterated to produce more fashionable varieties. There were once some wonderful Shiraz wines from Australia, and Zinfandels from California, made from seventy- or eighty-year-old vines. There are now some excellent Carignan wines produced in Languedoc-Roussillon from equally old vines. It is tempting for growers to plant the universal Chardonnay and Cabernet worldwide; the wines are very easy to sell. But let us not forget the region's heritage. It takes a minimum of ten to twenty years for a vine to produce top-quality wine, and a whole lifetime for it to produce outstanding wine. Will their grandchildren's inheritance be vines that have been carefully selected to suit both climate and soil, or will they live in ignorance of the highly individual styles and flavours of Languedoc-Roussillon which made the region famous before phylloxera?

Bibliography

Alain Berger and Frederic Maurel, *La Viticulture et l'Économie du Languedoc du XVIII siècle a nos Jours*, Éditions du Faubourg, 1980.

Louis Camo, Joseph Deloncle, Jacques Fanet, Yves Hoffmann, Pierre Ponsiou and Alfred Sauvy, *Les Vins du Roussillon*, Éditions Montalba, 1980.

Jean Clavel and Robert Baillaud, *Histoire et Avenir des Vins en Languedoc*, Éditions Privat, 1985.

Guy Deluchey, *Le Guide des Vins de Pays*, Marabout, 1985.

Roger Dion, *Histoire de la Vigne et du Vin en France des Origines au XIX siècle*, Flammarion, 1977.

Henri Enjalbert, *Un Vignoble de Qualité en Languedoc*, Imprimerie Chalaguier, 1985.

Joseph Fonquernie and Robert Euvrard, *La France Viti-vinicole*, Centre Régional de Documentation Pédagogique de l'Académie de Dijon, 1981.

Herbert Got, *Les Vins Doux Naturels*, Perpignan, 1947.

A. Huetz de Lemps, R. Pijassou and Philippe Roudié, *Géographie Historique des Vignobles*, Éditions du Centre National de la Recherche Scientifique, 1978.

Andre Jullien, *Topographie de Tous les Vignobles Connus* (1866), Champion-Statkine, 1985.

P. Morton Shand, *A Book of French Wines* (1928), Penguin, 1964.

Gérard Sanchez, *L'Hérault, Ses Sites, Ses Vins*, Les Presses du Languedoc, 1980.

Sur les Chemins des Vignobles de France, Selection Readers' Digest, 1984.

Fernand Woutaz, *Dictionnaire des Appellations de Tous les Vins de France*, Marabout, 1986.

Glossary

Cépages Améliorateurs
A variety which is recommended by the authorities to improve the quality within a region. Often part of a blend, giving improved colour, aroma and flavour to the wine.

Cordon de Royat
Training method for vines, whereby the vine has a permanent trunk with one or more permanent 'arms'. The new growth is from buds along the arms of the vine.

Coulure
Poor flower set in the vine, leading to fewer grapes developing on each bunch, and therefore a lower yield. Often caused by bad weather at the time of flowering: too hot, too cold, wet or windy. Can be caused by the vine's poor health or nutrition. Some vine varieties are particularly prone to coulure.

Ecimage
The removal of the shooting tips of the vine after flowering, to concentrate the vine's energy onto the flowers.

Effeuillage
The removal of some of the vine's leaves to allow better air circulation, and to allow sunlight to penetrate the vine's canopy. Also known as leaf plucking.

Epamprage
The removal of non-productive suckers shooting from the main trunk to prevent these from diverting energy from the main shoots.

Evantail
Method of training vines, whereby the vine is shaped like a fan, with the arms spreading fan-like from a central trunk.

Gobelet
Method of training vines, whereby the vine is shaped like a small bush, with the arms radiating upwards and outwards from a central trunk, in the shape of a cup or goblet.

Gourmands
Non-productive shoots appearing from the vine's main trunk. These shoots seldom bear many grapes, and divert energy from the main shoots.

Gris de Gris
Style of pale rosé wine where the grape skins are left in contact with the juice just long enough to give a hint of colour to the wine.

Guyot
Method of training vines on wires, whereby only the vine trunk is permanent. The fruiting branches are retained from the previous year's growth and trained along wires. A new branch is selected each year, and the previous year's branch is removed.

Macération Carbonique
Method of red wine vinification, also known as *vinification en grains entiers*, or whole grape vinification. This method extracts colour without extracting too much tannin, and gives a deep coloured but soft flavoured wine which can be drunk young.

Macération Pelliculaire
The process of leaving grape skins in contact with the grape juice, to extract some of the flavour compounds found in the skins. Usually associated with white wine production, especially with aromatic varieties such as muscat or sauvignon.

Marcottage
Vine multiplication by burying the tip of a vine until it has formed roots and become a separate vine. The most commonly used method before *phylloxera*.

Méthode Champenoise
The Champagne method of producing sparkling wines by secondary fermentation in the bottle.

Mistelle
An apéritif style wine produced from grape juice muted with alcohol.

Oïdium
Also known as powdery mildew. A fungal disease of the vine, giving a powdery appearance to the afected parts, and arresting vine growth and grape development.

Passerillage
A method of drying the ripe grapes on the vines, to evaporate part of the water content, and concentrate the sugars.

Phylloxera
An aphid which attacks vine roots and stems. Introduced from America in the 1800s, and combatted by the use of American vines (which are immune) for grafting.

Primeur
A style of wine for drinking young and fresh, in the year of its production. Also known as Nouveau.

Quitchage
A practiuce in Languedoc in the last century, whereby grapes would be pressed down in the collecting buckets, in order to cram the maximum amount into each bucket.

Rancio
A wine that has been aged in a cask or bonbonne until it has acquired a special 'old', almost caramelised flavour.

Rimage
A designation for a red Vin Doux Naturel that has been bottled young. Also known as Vintage.

Rognage
The thinning of shoots and leaves to allow better aeration of the vine, for the penetration of both sunlight and preventive sprays. Some grape bunches may also be removed to regulate the yield. Rognage is also used to facilitate picking, by removing shoots or leaves in the immediate vicinity of the grape bunches.

Saignée
A rosé wine produced from the first free run juice of red grapes. The 'bleeding' of these grapes leaves less juice in ratio to the skins for the production of red wine, and thereby concentrates the colour in the red.

Teinturier
A grape variety that has coloured juice. (Most varieties have colourless juice.)

Vin de Liqueur
A sweet fortified wine, generally less rich than a Vin Doux Naturel.

Vin Cuit
A sweet wine made from grape juice which has been concentrated by boiling.

Vin Nouveau
A style of wine for drinking young and fresh, in the year of its production. Also known as Primeur.

Vitis Vinifera
The Latin name for the family of grape vines which produce all the quality wines of the world.

Index